THE DOCTRINES

AND

DISCIPLINE

OF THE

METHODIST EPISCOPAL CHURCH.

Cincinnati:
PUBLISHED BY SWORMSTEDT & POE,
Corner of Main and Eighth streets.

R. P. THOMPSON, PRINTER.
1854.

TO THE MEMBERS

OF THE

METHODIST EPISCOPAL CHURCH.

Dearly Beloved Brethren,—We think it expedient to give you a brief account of the rise of Methodism, both in Europe and America. "In 1729, two young men, in England, reading the Bible, saw they could not be saved without holiness: followed after it, and incited others so to do. In 1737, they saw, likewise, that men are justified before they are sanctified: but still holiness was their object. God then thrust them out to raise a holy people."*

In the year 1766, Philip Embury, a local preacher of our society, from Ireland, began to preach in the city of

* These are the words of Messrs. Wesley themselves.

New-York, and formed a society of his own countrymen and the citizens; and the same year, Thomas Webb preached in a hired room near the barracks. About the same time, Robert Strawbridge, a local preacher from Ireland, settled in Frederick county, in the state of Maryland, and, preaching there, formed some societies. The first Methodist church was built in New-York in 1768 or 1769; and in 1769 Richard Boardman and Joseph Pilmoor came to New-York; who were the first regular Methodist preachers on the continent. In the latter end of the year 1771, Francis Asbury and Richard Wright, of the same order, came over.

We believe that God's design in raising up the preachers called Methodists in America, was to reform the continent, and spread Scripture holiness over these lands. As a proof hereof, we have seen, since that time, a great and glorious work of God, from New-York, through the Jersey, Pennsylvania, Delaware, Maryland, Virginia, North and South Carolina, and Georgia; as also, of late, to the extremities of the western and eastern states.

We esteem it our duty and privilege most earnestly to recommend to *you*, as members of our Church, our FORM OF DISCIPLINE, which has been founded on the experience of a long series of years; as also on the observations and remarks we have made on ancient and modern Churches.

We wish to see this little publication in the house of every Methodist; and the more so, as it contains the articles of religion maintained more or less, in part or in whole, by every reformed Church in the world.

Far from wishing you to be ignorant of any of our doctrines, or any part of our discipline, we desire you to read, mark, learn, and inwardly digest, the whole. You ought, next to the word of God, to procure the articles and canons of the Church to which you belong. This present edition is small and cheap, and we can assure you that the profits of the sale of it shall be applied to cha ritable and religious purposes.

We remain your very affectionate brethren and pastors, who labour night and day, both in public and in private, for your good.

BEVERLY WAUGH,
THOMAS A. MORRIS,
EDMUND S. JANES,
LEVI SCOTT,
MATTHEW SIMPSON,
EDWARD R. AMES,
OSMAN C. BAKER.

CONTENTS.

PART I.

ORIGIN, DOCTRINES, AND ADMINISTRATIVE RULES.

CHAPTER I.

ORIGIN AND ARTICLES.

CHAPTER II.

GENERAL RULES, AND RECEPTION OF MEMBERS.

CHAPTER III.

OF THE CONFERENCES.

CHAPTER IV.

OF THE MINISTERS.

CHAPTER V.

OF THE MEANS OF GRACE.

CHAPTER VI.

OF THE INSTRUCTION OF CHILDREN.

CHAPTER VII.

OF THE PRINTING AND CIRCULATION OF RELIGIOUS TRACTS.

CHAPTER VIII.

OF DRESS AND MARRIAGE.

CHAPTER IX.

OF BRINGING MINISTERS AND MEMBERS TO TRIAL, AND OF THE SETTLEMENT OF DISPUTES.

PART II.

THE RITUAL.

CHAPTER I.

THE ORDER OF BAPTISM.

CHAPTER II.

THE LORD'S SUPPER.

CHAPTER III.

FORMS OF ORDINATION.

CHAPTER IV.

THE FORM OF SOLEMNIZATION OF MATRIMONY.

CHAPTER V.

ORDER OF THE BURIAL OF THE DEAD.

PART III.

TEMPORAL ECONOMY.

CHAPTER I.

OF THE BOUNDARIES OF THE ANNUAL CONFERENCES.

CHAPTER II.

OF CHURCHES AND CHURCH PROPERTY.

CHAPTER III.

OF SUPPORT AND SUPPLIES.

CHAPTER IV.

THE SUPPORT OF MISSIONS.

CHAPTER V.

OF THE CHARTERED FUND.

CHAPTER VI.

PRINTING AND CIRCULATING OF BOOKS.

CHAPTER VII.

OF SLAVERY.

THE

DOCTRINES AND DISCIPLINE

OF THE

METHODIST E. CHURCH.

PART I.

Origin, Doctrines, and Administrative Rules.

CHAPTER I.

ORIGIN AND ARTICLES.

SECTION I.

Of the Origin of the Methodist E. Church.

THE preachers and members of our society in general, being convinced that there was a great deficiency of vital religion in the Church of England in America, and being in many places destitute of the Christian sacraments, as several of the clergy had forsaken their churches, requested the late Rev. *John Wesley* to take such measures, in his wisdom and prudence, as would afford them suitable relief in their distress.

In consequence of this, our venerable friend, who, under God, had been the father of the great revival of religion now extending over the earth, by the means of the

Methodists, determined to ordain ministers for America; and for this purpose, in the year 1784, sent over three regularly ordained clergy: but preferring the episcopal mode of Church government to any other, he solemnly set apart, by the imposition of his hands and prayer, one of them, namely, *Thomas Coke*, Doctor of Civil Law, late of Jesus College, in the University of Oxford, and a presbyter of the Church of England, for the episcopal office; and having delivered to him letters of episcopal orders, commissioned and directed him to set apart *Francis Asbury*, then general assistant of the Methodist Society in America, for the same episcopal office; he, the said *Francis Asbury*, being first ordained deacon and elder. In consequence of which, the said *Francis Asbury* was solemnly set apart for the said episcopal office by prayer, and the imposition of the hands of the said *Thomas Coke*, other regularly ordained ministers assisting in the sacred ceremony. At which time the General Conference, held at Baltimore, did unanimously receive the said *Thomas Coke* and *Francis Asbury* as their bishops, being fully satisfied of the validity of their episcopal ordination.

SECTION II.

ARTICLES OF RELIGION.

I. *Of Faith in the Holy Trinity.*

THERE is but one living and true God, everlasting, without body or parts, of infinite power, wisdom, and goodness: the maker and preserver of all things, visible and invisible. And in unity of this Godhead, there are three persons, of one substance, power, and eternity;—the Father, the Son, and the Holy Ghost.

II. *Of the Word, or Son of God, who was made very Man.*

The Son, who is the Word of the Father, the very and eternal God, of one substance with the Father, took man's nature in the womb of the blessed virgin; so that two whole and perfect natures, that is to say, the Godhead and manhood, were joined together in one person, never to be divided, whereof is one Christ, very God and very man, who truly suffered, was crucified, dead and buried, to reconcile his Father to us, and to be a sacrifice, not only for original guilt, but also for actual sins of men.

III. *Of the Resurrection of Christ.*

Christ did truly rise again from the dead, and took again his body, with all things appertaining to the perfection of man s nature, wherewith he ascended into heaven, and there sitteth until he return to judge all men at the last day.

IV. *Of the Holy Ghost.*

The Holy Ghost, proceeding from the Father and the Son, is of one substance, majesty, and glory, with the Father and the Son, very and eternal God.

V. *The Sufficiency of the Holy Scriptures for Salvation.*

The Holy Scriptures contain all things necessary to salvation: so that whatsoever is not read therein, nor may be proved thereby, is not to be required of any man, that it should be believed as an article of faith, or be thought requisite or necessary to salvation. In the name of the Holy Scripture, we do understand those canonical books of the Old and New Testament, of whose authority was never any doubt in the Church.

The Names of the Canonical Books.

Genesis,
Exodus,
Leviticus,
Numbers,
Deuteronomy,
Joshua,
Judges,
Ruth,
The First Book of Samuel,
The Second Book of Samuel,

The First Book of Kings,
The Second Book of Kings,
The First Book of Chronicles,
The Second Book of Chronicles,
The Book of Ezra,
The Book of Nehemiah,
The Book of Esther,
The Book of Job,
The Psalms,
The Proverbs,
Ecclesiastes, or the Preacher,
Cantica, or Songs of Solomon,
Four Prophets the greater,
Twelve Prophets the less:

All the books of the New Testament, as they are commonly received, we do receive and account canonical.

VI. *Of the Old Testament.*

The Old Testament is not contrary to the New; for both in the Old and New Testament everlasting life is offered to mankind by Christ, who is the only Mediator between God and man, being both God and man. Wherefore they are not to be heard who feign that the old fathers did look only for transitory promises. Although the law given from God by Moses, as touching ceremonies and rites, doth not bind Christians, nor ought the civil precepts thereof of necessity be received in any commonwealth; yet, notwithstanding, no Christian whatsoever is free from the obedience of the commandments which are called moral.

VII. *Of Original or Birth Sin.*

Original sin standeth not in the following of Adam, (as the Pelagians do vainly talk,) but it is the corruption of the nature of every man, that naturally is engendered of the offspring of Adam, whereby man is very far gone from original righteousness, and of his own nature inclined to evil, and that continually.

VIII. *Of Free Will.*

The condition of man after the fall of Adam is such, that he cannot turn and prepare himself, by his own natural strength and works, *to faith, and calling upon God; wherefore* we have no power to do good works, pleasant and acceptable to God, without the grace of God by Christ preventing us, that we may have a good will, and working with us, when we have that good will.

IX. *Of the Justification of Man.*

We are accounted righteous before God, only for the merit of our Lord and Saviour Jesus Christ by faith, and not for our own works or deservings:—Wherefore, that we are justified by faith only, is a most wholesome doctrine, and very full of comfort.

X. *Of Good Works.*

Although good works, which are the fruits of faith, and follow after justification, cannot put away our sins, and endure the severity of God's judgments; yet are they pleasing and acceptable to God in Christ, and spring out of a true and lively faith, insomuch that by them a lively faith may be as evidently known as a tree is discerned by its fruit.

XI. *Of Works of Supererogation.*

Voluntary works,—besides, over, and above God's commandments—which are called works of supererogation, cannot be taught without arrogancy and impiety. For by them men do declare that they do not only render unto God as much as they are bound to do, but that they do more for his sake than of bounden duty is required: whereas Christ saith plainly, When ye have done all that is commanded you, say, We are unprofitable servants.

XII. *Of Sin after Justification.*

Not every sin willingly committed after justification is the sin against the Holy Ghost, and unpardonable. Wherefore, the grant of repentance is not to be denied to such as fall into sin after justification: after we have received the Holy Ghost, we may depart from grace given, and fall into sin, and, by the grace of God, rise again and amend our lives. And therefore they are to be condemned who say they can no more sin as long as they live here: or deny the place of forgiveness to such as truly repent.

XIII. *Of the Church.*

The visible Church of Christ is a congregation of faithful men, in which the pure word of God is preached, and the sacraments duly administered, according to Christ's ordinance, in all those things that of necessity are requisite to the same.

XIV. *Of Purgatory.*

The Romish doctrine concerning purgatory, pardon, worshipping, and adoration, as well of images as of relics, and also invocation of saints, is a fond thing, vainly invented, and grounded upon no warrant of Scripture, but repugnant to the word of God.

XV. *Of speaking in the Congregation in such a Tongue as the People understand.*

It is a thing plainly repugnant to the word of God, and the custom of the primitive Church, to have public prayer in the Church, or to minister the sacraments, in a tongue not understood by the people.

XVI. *Of the Sacraments.*

Sacraments, ordained of Christ, are not only badges or tokens of Christian men's profession; but rather they are certain signs of grace, and God's good-will toward us, by the which he doth work invisibly in us, and doth not only quicken, but also strengthen and confirm our faith in him.

There are two sacraments ordained of Christ our Lord in the gospel; that is to say, baptism and the supper of the Lord.

Those five commonly called sacraments, that is to say, confirmation, penance, orders, matrimony, and extreme unction, are not to be counted for sacraments of the gospel, being such as have partly grown out of the *corrupt* following of the apostles; and partly are states of life allowed in the Scriptures, but yet have not the like nature of baptism and the Lord's supper, because they have not any visible sign or ceremony ordained of God.

The sacraments were not ordained of Christ to be gazed upon, or to be carried about; but that we should duly use them. And in such only as worthily receive the same, they have a wholesome effect or operation: but they that receive them unworthily, purchase to themselves condemnation, as St. Paul saith, 1 Cor. xi, 29.

XVII. *Of Baptism.*

Baptism is not only a sign of profession, and mark of difference, whereby Christians are distinguished from others that are not baptized: but it is also a sign of regeneration, or the new birth. The baptism of young children is to be retained in the Church.

XVIII. *Of the Lord's Supper.*

The supper of the Lord is not only a sign of the love that Christians ought to have among themselves one to another, but rather is a sacrament of our redemption by Christ's death; insomuch that, to such as rightly, worthily, and with faith receive the same, the bread which we break is a partaking of the body of Christ; and likewise the cup of blessing is a partaking of the blood of Christ.

Transubstantiation, or the change of the substance of bread and wine in the supper of our Lord, cannot be proved by Holy Writ, but is repugnant to the plain words of Scripture, overthroweth the nature of a sacrament, and hath given occasion to many superstitions.

The body of Christ is given, taken, and eaten in the supper, only after a heavenly and spiritual manner. And the means whereby the body of Christ is received and eaten in the supper, is faith.

The sacrament of the Lord's supper was not by Christ's ordinance reserved, carried about, lifted up, or worshipped.

XIX. *Of both kinds.*

The cup of the Lord is not to be denied to the lay people: for both the parts of the Lord's supper, by Christ's ordinance and commandment, ought to be administered to all Christians alike.

XX. *Of the one Oblation of Christ, finished upon the Cross.*

The offering of Christ, once made, is that perfect redemption, propitiation, and satisfaction for all the sins of the whole world, both original and actual: and there is none other satisfaction for sin but that alone. Wherefore the sacrifice of masses, in the which it is commonly said that the priest doth offer Christ for the quick and the dead, to have remission of pain or guilt, is a blasphemous fable, and dangerous deceit.

XXI. *Of the Marriage of Ministers.*

The ministers of Christ are not commanded by God's law either to vow the estate of single life, or to abstain from marriage: therefore it is lawful for them, as for all other Christians, to marry at their own discretion, as they shall judge the same to serve best to godliness.

XXII. *Of the Rites and Ceremonies of Churches.*

It is not necessary that rites and ceremonies should in all places be the same, or exactly alike; for they have been always different, and may be changed according to the diversity of countries, times, and men's manners, so that nothing be ordained against God's word. Whosoever, through his private judgment, willingly and purposely doth openly break the rites and ceremonies of the Church to which he belongs, which are not repugnant to the word of God, and are ordained and approved by common authority, ought to be rebuked openly, that others may fear to do the like, as one that offendeth against the common order of the Church, and woundeth the consciences of weak brethren.

Every particular Church may ordain, change, or abolish, rites and ceremonies, so that all things may be done to edification

XXIII. *Of the Rulers of the United States of America.*

The president, the congress, the general assemblies, the governors, and the councils of state, *as the delegates of the people*, are the rulers of the United States of America, according to the division of power made to them by the constitution of the United States, and by the constitutions of their respective states. And the said states are a sovereign and independent nation, and ought not to be subject to any foreign jurisdiction.*

XXIV. *Of Christian Men's Goods.*

The riches and goods of Christians are not common, as touching the right, title, and possession of the same, as some do falsely boast. Notwithstanding, every man ought,

* As far as it respects civil affairs, we believe it the duty of Christians, and especially all Christian ministers, to be subject to the supreme authority of the country where they may reside, and to use all laudable means to enjoin obedience to the powers that be; and therefore it is expected that all our preachers and people, who may be under the British, or any other government, will behave themselves as peaceable and orderly subjects.

of such things as he possesseth, liberally to give alms to the poor, according to his ability.

XXV. *Of a Christian Man's Oath.*

As we confess that vain and rash swearing is forbidden Christian men by our Lord Jesus Christ and James his apostle; so we judge that the Christian religion doth not prohibit, but that a man may swear when the magistrate requireth, in a cause of faith and charity, so it be done according to the prophet's teaching, in justice, judgment, and truth.

CHAPTER II.

GENERAL RULES, AND RECEPTION OF MEMBERS.

SECTION I.

The Nature, Design, and General Rules of our United Societies.

(1) In the latter end of the year 1739, eight or ten persons came to Mr. Wesley in London, who appeared to be deeply convinced of sin, and earnestly groaning for redemption. They desired (as did two or three more the next day) that he would spend some time with them in prayer, and advise them how to flee from the wrath to come; which they saw continually hanging

over their heads. That he might have more time for this great work, he appointed a day when they might all come together; which from thenceforward they did every week, namely, on *Thursday*, in the evening. To these, and as many more as desired to join with them, (for their number increased daily,) he gave those advices from time to time which he judged most needful for them; and they always concluded their meeting with prayer suited to their several necessities.

(2) This was the rise of the UNITED SOCIETY, first in *Europe*, and then in *America*. Such a society is no other than "*a company of men* having the form and seeking the power of *godliness, united in order to pray together, to receive the word of exhortation, and to watch over one another in love, that they may help each other to work out their salvation.*"

(3) That it may the more easily be discerned whether they are indeed working out their own salvation, each society is divided into smaller companies, called classes, according to their respective places of abode. There are about twelve persons in a class; one of whom is styled *the leader*. It is his duty,

I. To see each person in his class once a week at least; in order,

1. To inquire how their souls prosper.

2. To advise, reprove, comfort, or exhort, as occasion may require.

3. To receive what they are willing to

give toward the relief of the preachers, church, and poor.*

II. To meet the ministers and the stewards of the society once a week; in order,

1. To inform the minister of any that are sick, or of any that walk disorderly, and will not be reproved.

2. To pay the stewards what they have received of their several classes in the week preceding.

(4) There is only one condition previously required of those who desire admission into these societies, "a desire to flee from the wrath to come, and to be saved from their sins." But wherever this is really fixed in the soul, it will be shown by its fruits. It is therefore expected of all who continue therein, that they should continue to evidence their desire of salvation,

First, By doing no harm, by avoiding evil of every kind, especially that which is most generally practiced; such as,

The taking of the name of God in vain.

The profaning the day of the Lord, either by doing ordinary work therein, or by buying or selling.

Drunkenness, buying or selling spirituous liquors, or drinking them, unless in cases of extreme necessity.

The buying and selling of men, women, and children, with an intention to enslave them.

Fighting, quarrelling, brawling, brother

* This part refers to towns and cities; where the poor are generally numerous, and church expenses considerable.

going to law with brother; returning evil for evil; or railing for railing; the *using many words* in buying or selling.

The *buying or selling goods that have not paid the duty.*

The *giving or taking things on usury,* i. e., unlawful interest.

Uncharitable or *unprofitable* conversation; particularly speaking evil of magistrates or of ministers.

Doing to others as we would not they should do unto us.

Doing what we know is not for the glory of God: as,

The *putting on of gold and costly apparel.*

The *taking such diversions* as cannot be used in the name of the Lord Jesus.

The *singing* those *songs,* or *reading* those *books,* which do not tend to the knowledge or love of God.

Softness and needless self-indulgence.

Laying up treasure upon earth.

Borrowing without a probability of paying; or taking up goods without a probability of paying for them.

(5) It is expected of all who continue in these societies, that they should continue to evidence their desire of salvation,

Secondly, By doing good, by being in every kind merciful after their power, as they have opportunity, doing good of every possible sort, and, as far as possible, to all men.

To their bodies, of the ability which God giveth, by giving food to the hungry, by clothing the naked, by visiting or helping them that are sick or in prison.

To their souls, by instructing, reproving, or exhorting all we have any intercourse with; trampling under foot that enthusiastic doctrine, that "we are not to do good unless *our hearts be free to it.*"

By doing good, especially to them that are of the household of faith, or groaning so to be; employing them preferably to others, buying one of another, helping each other in business; and so much the more because the world will love its own, and them *only.*

By all possible *diligence* and *frugality*, that the gospel be not blamed.

By running with patience the race which is set up before them, *denying themselves, and taking up their cross daily;* submitting to bear the reproach of Christ, to be as the filth and offscouring of the world; and looking that men should say *all manner of evil of them falsely for the Lord's sake.*

(6) It is expected of all who desire to continue in these societies, that they should continue to evidence their desire of salvation,

Thirdly, By attending upon all the ordinances of God: such are,

The public worship of God:

The ministry of the word, either read or expounded:

The supper of the Lord:

Family and private prayer:

Searching the Scriptures, and

Fasting or abstinence.

(7) These are the general rules of our societies: all which we are taught of God to observe, even in his written word, which is the only rule, and the sufficient rule both of our faith and practice. And all these we know his Spirit writes on truly awakened hearts. If there be any among us who observe them not, who habitually break any of them, let it be known unto them who watch over that soul, as they who must give an account. We will admonish him of the error of his ways. We will bear with him for a season. But if then he repent not, he hath no more place among us. We have delivered our own souls.

SECTION II.

Of Receiving Members into the Church.

Quest. 1. How shall we prevent improper persons from insinuating themselves into the Church?

Answ. 1. *Let none be received into the Church until they are recommended by a leader with whom they have met at least six months on trial, and have been baptized; and shall on examination by the minister in charge, before the Church, give satisfactory assurances both of the correctness of their faith, and their willingness to observe and keep the rules of the Church.* Nevertheless, if a member in good standing in any other orthodox Church shall desire to unite with us, such applicant may, by giving satisfactory answers to the usual inquiries, be received at once into full fellowship.

2. Let none be admitted on trial, except they are well recommended by one you know, or until they have met twice or thrice in class.

3. Read the rules to them the first time they meet.

Quest. 2. How shall we be more exact in receiving and excluding members?

Answ. The official minister or preacher shall, at every quarterly meeting, read the names of those that are received into the Church, and also those that are excluded therefrom.

CHAPTER III.

OF THE CONFERENCES.

SECTION I.

Of our Deportment at the Conferences.

It is desired that all things be considered on these occasions as in the immediate presence of God: that every person speak freely whatever is in his heart.

Quest. How may we best improve our time at the conferences?

Answ. 1. While we are conversing, let us have an especial care to set God always before us.

2. In the intermediate hours, let us redeem all the time we can for private exercises.

3. Therein let us give ourselves to prayer for one another, and for a blessing on our labor.

SECTION II.

Of the General Conference.

Quest. Who shall compose the General Conference, and what are the regulations and powers belonging to it?

Answ. 1. The General Conference shall be composed of one member for every twenty-one members of each annual conference, to be appointed either by seniority or choice, at the discretion of such annual conference: yet so that such representatives shall have travelled at least four full calendar years from the time that they were received on trial by an annual conference, and are in full connextion at the time of holding the conference.

2. The General Conference shall meet on the first day of May, in the year of our Lord 1812, in the city of New-York, and thenceforward on the first day of May once in four years perpetually, in such place or places as shall be fixed on by the General Conference from time to time: but the general superintendents, with or by the advice of all the annual conferences, or if there be no general superintendent, all the annual conferences respectively, shall have power to call a General Conference, if they judge it necessary, at any time.

3. At all times when the General Conference is met, it shall take two-thirds of the

representatives of all the annual conferences to make a quorum for transacting business.

4. One of the general superintendents shall preside in the General Conference; but in case no general superintendent be present, the General Conference shall choose a president pro tem.

5. The General Conference shall have full powers to make rules and regulations for our Church, under the following limitations and restrictions, namely:—

1. The General Conference shall not revoke, alter, or change our articles of religion, nor establish any new standards or rules of doctrine contrary to our present existing and established standards of doctrine.
2. They shall not allow of more than one representative for every fourteen members of the annual conference, nor allow of a less number than one for every thirty: provided, nevertheless, that when there shall be in any annual conference a fraction of two-thirds the number which shall be fixed for the ratio of representation, such annual conference shall be entitled to an additional delegate for such fraction; and provided, also, that no conference shall be denied the privilege of two delegates.
3. They shall not change or alter any part or rule of our government, so as to do away episcopacy, or destroy the plan of our itinerant general superintendency.
4. They shall not revoke or change the general rules of the United Societies.

5. They shall not do away the privileges of our ministers or preachers of trial by a committee, and of an appeal: neither shall they do away the privileges of our members of trial before the society, or by a committee, and of an appeal.
6. They shall not appropriate the produce of the Book Concern, nor of the Charter Fund, to any purpose other than for the benefit of the travelling, supernumerary, superannuated and worn-out preachers, their wives, widows, and children. *Provided*, nevertheless, that upon the concurrent recommendation of three-fourths of all the members of the several Annual Conferences, who shall be present and vote on such recommendation, then a majority of two-thirds of the General Conference succeeding shall suffice to alter any of the above restrictions, excepting the first article: and also, whenever such alteration or alterations shall have been first recommended by two-thirds of the General Conference, so soon as three-fourths of the members of all the Annual Conferences shall have concurred as aforesaid, such alteration or alterations shall take effect.

SECTION III.

Of the Annual Conferences.

Quest. 1. Who shall attend the Annual Conferences?

Answ. All the travelling preachers—both

those who are in full connexion, and those who are on trial.

Quest. 2. Who shall appoint the times of holding the Annual Conferences?

Answ. The Bishops: but they shall allow the Annual Conferences to sit a week at least.

Quest. 3. Who shall appoint the places of holding the Annual Conferences?

Answ. Each Annual Conference shall appoint the place of its own sitting.

Quest. 4. Who shall preside at the Annual Conferences?

Answ. The Bishop. In case no Bishop be present, a Presiding Elder, appointed by a Bishop, by letter or otherwise, shall preside. But if no appointment be made, or if the Presiding Elder appointed do not attend, the Conference shall in either of these cases elect the President by ballot, without a debate, from among the Presiding Elders.

Quest. 5. What is the method wherein we usually proceed in the Annual Conferences?

Answ. We inquire,

1. What preachers are admitted on trial?
2. Who remain on trial?
3. Who are admitted into full connexion?
4. Who are the Deacons?
5. Who have been elected and ordained Elders this year?
6. Who have located this year?
7. Who are the supernumeraries?
8. Who are the superannuated or worn-out preachers?

9. Who have been expelled from the connexion this year?
10. Who have withdrawn from the connexion this year?
11. Are all the preachers blameless in life and conversation?
12. Who have died this year?
13. What is the number of members, and what of probationers, in society?
14. What amounts are necessary for the superannuated preachers, and the widows and orphans of preachers, and to make up the deficiencies of those who have not obtained their regular allowance on the circuits?
15. What has been collected on the foregoing accounts, and how has it been applied?
16. What has been contributed for the support of Missions, what for the Sunday-School Union, what for the publication and circulation of tracts, and what to aid the American Bible Society?
17. Where are the preachers stationed this year?
18. Where and when shall our next Conference be held?

Quest. 6. Is there any other business to be done in the Annual Conferences?

Answ. 1. The electing and ordaining of Deacons and Elders.

2. It shall be the duty of each Annual Conference to examine strictly into the state of the domestic missions within its bounds, and to allow none to remain on the list of

its missions which, in the judgment of the Conference, is able to support itself.

Quest. 7. Are there any other directions to be given concerning the Annual Conferences?

Answ. There shall be thirty-nine Conferences in the year. (See part iii. ch. 1, page 158.)

A record of the proceedings of each Annual Conference shall be kept by a Secretary, chosen for that purpose, and shall be signed by the President and Secretary; and let a copy of the said record be sent to the General Conference.

☞ For other special duties of the Annual Conference, with reference to Missions, Sunday schools, and Tracts, see pages 190, 85, 87.

SECTION IV.

Of the Quarterly Conferences.

Quest. 1. Of whom shall the Quarterly Conferences be composed?

Answ. Of all the travelling and local preachers, exhorters, stewards, and class-leaders of the circuit or station, and none else. But the male superintendents of Sunday schools, being members of our Church, shall, by virtue of their office, have a seat in the Quarterly Conference having supervision of their schools, with the right to speak and vote on questions relating to Sunday schools, and on such questions only; and the Missionary Committee (part iii, ch. iv, page 191) shall have the right to a seat during the action of the Conference on the subject of Missions, but at no other time.

Quest. 2. Who shall preside in the Quarterly Conferences ?

Answ. The Presiding Elder, and in his absence the preacher in charge.

Quest. 3. How shall the minutes of the Quarterly Conference be kept ?

Answ. The Quarterly Conference shall appoint a Secretary to take down the proceedings thereof, in a book kept by one of the Stewards of the circuit for that purpose.

Quest. 4. What shall be the regular business *of the Quarterly Conference* ?

Answ. 1. To hear complaints, and to receive and try appeals.

2. To appoint a committee to make an estimate of the amount necessary to furnish fuel and table expenses for the family or families of the preacher or preachers of the circuit or station, which estimate shall be subject to the action of the Quarterly Conference. (See part iii, ch. iii, § 2, art. 6, page 180.)

3. To take cognizance of all the local preachers in the circuit or station, and to inquire into the gifts, labours, and usefulness, of each preacher by name; to license proper persons to preach, and renew their license annually, when in the judgment of said Conference their gifts, grace, and usefulness, will warrant such renewal; to recommend to the Annual Conference suitable candi-

dates in the local connexion for Deacons' or Elders' orders, and for admission on trial in the travelling connexion; and to try, suspend, expel, or acquit any local preacher in the circuit or station against whom charges may be brought. *Provided*, that no person shall be licensed to preach without the recommendation of the society of which he is a member, or of a leaders' meeting; nor shall any one be licensed to preach, or recommended to the Annual Conference to travel, or for ordination, without first being examined in the Quarterly Conference on the subject of doctrines and discipline. (See § 6, p. 49, and § 18, p. 75.)

4. To appoint Stewards, the preacher in charge having the right to nominate, (see part iii, ch. iii, § 4, quest. 2, p. 183, and quest. 4, p. 184;) and to examine the characters of exhorters annually, and recommend them, if approved, for renewal of license. (See part i, ch. iv, § 11, quest. 2, answ. 13, p. 62.)

5. To appoint District Stewards as provided for in part iii, ch. iii, § 2, ans. 2, p. 181, and a Parsonage Committee, if necessary. (See part iii, ch. iii, § 6, answ. 3, p. 189.)

6. To appoint a Missionary Committee, as provided for in part iii, ch. iv, art. 4, p. 191.

7. To receive the annual reports of Trustees, as provided for in part iii, ch. ii, § 3, art. 6, p. 177.

8. Each Quarterly Conference shall have supervision of all the Sunday schools and

Sunday-School Societies within its bounds. (See part i, ch. iv, § 11, quest. 1, answ. 19, p. 60; and ch. vi, answ. 1, p. 85.)

CHAPTER IV.

OF THE MINISTERS.

SECTION I.

Of the Election and Consecration of Bishops, and of their Duty.

Quest. 1. How is a Bishop to be constituted?

Answ. By the election of the General Conference, and the laying on of the hands of three Bishops, or at least of one Bishop and two Elders.

Quest. 2. If by death, expulsion, or otherwise, there be no Bishop remaining in our Church, what shall we do?

Answ. The General Conference shall elect a Bishop; and the Elders, or any three of them, who shall be appointed by the General Conference for that purpose, shall ordain him according to our form of ordination.

Quest. 3. What are the duties of a Bishop?

Answ. 1. To preside in our Conferences.

2. To form the districts according to his judgment.

3. To fix the appointments of the preachers, provided he shall not allow any preacher to remain in the same station more than two years successively; except the Presiding Elders, the Corresponding Secretary of the

Missionary Society, the Editors and Agents at New-York and Cincinnati; the Editors at Auburn, Pittsburgh, Chicago, St. Louis, and San Francisco; the supernumerary, superannuated and worn-out preachers, missionaries among the Indians, Welsh, Swedes, Norwegians, and other missionaries among foreigners, (not including the Germans,) where supplies are difficult to be obtained, missionaries to our people of colour and on foreign stations, chaplains to state prisons, and in the army or navy, those preachers that may be appointed to labour for the special benefit of seamen, and for the American Bible Society, also the preacher or preachers that may be stationed in the city of New-Orleans, and the presidents, principals, or teachers, of seminaries of learning, which are or may be under our superintendence; and also, when requested by an Annual Conference, to appoint a preacher for a longer time than two years to any seminary of learning not under our care: *provided*, also, that, with the exceptions above named, he shall not continue a preacher in the same appointment more than two years in six; nor in the same city more than four years in succession; nor return him to it, after such term of service, till he shall have been absent four years. He shall have authority, when requested by an Annual Conference, to appoint an agent, whose duty it shall be to travel throughout the bounds of such Conference, for the purpose of establishing and aiding Sabbath Schools, and distributing tracts, and also to appoint an agent or agents for the benefit of our literary institutions, and an agent for the German publishing fund.

4. In the intervals of the Conferences, to change, receive, and suspend preachers, as necessity may require, and as the Discipline directs.

5. To travel through the connexion at large.

6. To oversee the spiritual and temporal business of our Church.

7. To ordain Bishops, Elders, and Deacons.

8. To decide all questions of law in an Annual Conference, subject to an appeal to the General Conference; but in all cases the application of law shall be with the Conference.

9. To point out a course of reading and study, proper to be pursued by candidates for the ministry for the term of four years.

10. A Bishop may, when he judges it necessary, unite two or more circuits or stations together, without affecting their separate financial interests, or pastoral duties.

Quest. 4. If a Bishop cease from travelling at large among the people, shall he still exercise his episcopal office among us in any degree?

Answ. If he cease from travelling without the consent of the General Conference, he shall not thereafter exercise the episcopal office in our Church.

Quest. 5. What shall be done when there is no bishop to travel at large?

Answ. In case there be no Bishop to travel through the districts and exercise the episcopal office, on account of death, or otherwise, the districts shall be regulated in every respect by the Annual Conferences and the Presiding Elders in the interval of General Conference, ordination excepted.

SECTION II.

Of the Presiding Elders, and of their Duty.

Quest. 1. By whom are the Presiding Elders to be chosen?

Answ. By the Bishops.

Quest. 2. By whom are the Presiding Elders to be stationed and changed?

Answ. By the Bishops.

Quest. 3. How long may a Bishop allow an Elder to preside in the same district?

Answ. For any term not exceeding four years; after which he shall not be appointed to the same district for six years.

Quest. 4. What are the duties of a Presiding Elder?

Answ. 1. To travel through his appointed district.

2. In the absence of the Bishop, to take charge of all the Elders and Deacons, travelling and local preachers, and exhorters, in his district.

3. To change, receive, and suspend preachers in his district during the intervals of the Conferences, and in the absence of the Bishop, as the Discipline directs.

4. In the absence of a Bishop, to preside

in the Conference. (See part i, ch. iii, § 3, quest. 4, p. 35.)

5. To be present at, as far as practicable, and to hold all the quarterly meetings; and to call together at each quarterly meeting, a Quarterly Conference, (see part i, ch. iii, § 4, p. 37,) consisting of all the travelling and local preachers, exhorters, stewards, and leaders of the circuit, and none else, to hear complaints, and to receive and try appeals, and to transact such other business as is provided for in part i, ch. iii, § 4, pages 38, 39.

6. To oversee the spiritual and temporal business of the Church in his district, (see page 189,) and to promote, by all proper means, the cause of Missions, (see page 191,) and Sunday Schools, (see page 85,) and the publication, at our own press, of Bibles, tracts, and Sunday-School Books; and carefully to inquire, at each Quarterly Conference, whether the rules respecting the instruction of children (see page 85) have been faithfully observed; and to report to the Annual Conference the names of all travelling preachers within his district who shall neglect to observe these rules.

7. To take care that every part of our Discipline be enforced in his district. And to decide all questions of law in a Quarterly Conference, subject to an appeal to the President of the next Annual Conference; but in all cases the application of law shall be with the Conference.

8. To attend the Bishops when present in his district; and to give them, when ab-

sent, all necessary information, by letter, of the state of his district.

9. To direct the candidates who are admitted on trial, to those studies which have been recommended by the Bishops.

10. To explain to those preachers who are on trial, as well as to those who are in future to be proposed for trial, that they may be either admitted, or rejected without doing them any wrong.

11. If any preacher absent himself from his circuit, the Presiding Elder shall, as far as possible, fill his place with another preacher, who shall be paid for his labours out of the allowance of the absent preacher, in proportion to his usual allowance.

Quest. 5. Shall the Presiding Elder have power to employ a preacher who has been rejected at the previous Annual Conference?

Answ. He shall not, unless the Conference should give him liberty, under certain conditions.

SECTION III.

Of the Election and Ordination of Travelling Elders, and of their Duty.

Quest. 1. How is an Elder constituted?

Answ. By the election of a majority of the Annual Conference, and by the laying on of the hands of a Bishop, and some of the Elders that are present.

Quest. 2. What is the duty of a Travelling Elder?

Answ. 1. To administer baptism and the

Lord's supper, and to perform the office of matrimony, and all parts of divine worship.

2. To do all the duties of a travelling preacher.

No Elder that ceases to travel, without the consent of the Annual Conference, certified under the hand of the President of the Conference, except in case of sickness, debility, or other unavoidable circumstances, shall on any account, exercise the peculiar functions of his office, or even be allowed to preach among us: *nevertheless*, the final determination in all such cases is with the Annual Conference.

Quest. 3. What shall be the time of probation of a Travelling Deacon for the office of an Elder?

Answ. Every Travelling Deacon shall exercise that office for two years, before he be eligible to the office of Elder; except in the case of missions, when the Annual Conferences shall have authority to elect for the Elder's office sooner, if they judge it expedient.

When a preacher shall have passed his examination, and been admitted into full connexion, and elected to Deacon's office, but fails of his ordination through the absence of the Bishop, his eligibility to the office of Elder shall run from the time of his election to the office of a Deacon.

SECTION IV.

Of the Election and Ordination of Travelling Deacons, and of their Duty.

Quest. 1. How is a Travelling Deacon constituted?

Answ. By the election of a majority of the Annual Conference, and the laying on of the hands of a Bishop.

Quest. 2. What is the duty of a Travelling Deacon?

Answ. 1. To baptize and perform the office of matrimony, in the absence of the Elder.

2. To assist the Elder in administering the Lord's supper.

3. To do all the duties of a travelling preacher.

N. B. Whenever a preacher on trial is selected by the Bishop for a mission, he may, if elected by an Annual Conference, ordain him a Deacon before his probation ends.

No Deacon who ceases to travel without the consent of the Annual Conference, certified under the hand of the President of the Conference, except in case of sickness, debility, or other unavoidable circumstances, shall on any account, exercise the peculiar functions of his office, or even be allowed to preach among us: *nevertheless*, the final determination in all such cases is with the Annual Conference.

SECTION V.

Of the Reception of Preachers from the Wesleyan Connexion, and from other Denominations.

Quest. 1. In what manner shall we receive those ministers who may come to us from the Wesleyan connexion in Europe or Canada?

Answ. If they come to us properly accredited from either the British, Irish, or Canada Conference, they may be received according to such credentials, provided they give satisfaction to an Annual Conference of their willingness to conform to our Church government and usages.

Quest. 2. How shall we receive those ministers who may offer to unite with us from other Christian Churches?

Answ. Those ministers of other evangelical Churches, who may desire to unite with our Church, whether as local or itinerant, may be received according to our usages, on condition of their taking upon them our ordination vows, without the re-imposition of hands, giving satisfaction to an Annual Conference of their being in orders, and of their agreement with us in doctrine, discipline, government, and usages: *provided* the Conference is also satisfied with their gifts, grace, and usefulness. Whenever any such minister is received, he shall be furnished with a certificate, signed by one of our Bishops, in the following words, namely:—

This is to certify, that has been admitted into Conference as a travelling preacher, [or has been admitted as a local preacher on circuit,] he having been ordained to the office of Deacon, [or an Elder, as the case may be,] according to the usages of the Church, of which he has been a member and minister; and he is hereby authorized to exercise the functions pertaining to his office in the Methodist Episcopal Church, so long as his life and conversation are such as become the gospel of Christ.

Given under my hand and seal, at , this day of , in the year of our Lord .

Quest. 3. How shall we receive preachers of other denominations who are not in orders?

Answ. They may be received as licentiates, provided they give satisfaction to a Quarterly or an Annual Conference that they are suitable persons to exercise the office, and of their agreement with the doctrines, discipline, government, and usages of our Church.

SECTION VI.

Of the Examination of those who think they are moved by the Holy Ghost to preach.

Quest. How shall we try those who profess to be moved by the Holy Ghost to preach?

Answ. 1. Let the following questions be asked, namely:—Do they know God as a pardoning God? Have they the love of God abiding in them? Do they desire nothing but God? And are they holy in all manner of conversation?

2. Have they gifts (as well as grace) for the work? Have they (in some tolerable degree) a clear, sound understanding, a right judgment in the things of God, a just conception of salvation by faith? And has God given them any degree of utterance? Do they speak justly, readily, clearly?

3. Have they fruit? Are any truly convinced of sin, and converted to God by their preaching?

As long as these three marks concur in any one, we believe he is called of God to preach. These we receive as sufficient proof that he is moved by the Holy Ghost.

SECTION VII.

Of the Method of Receiving Travelling Preachers on Trial.

Quest. How is a preacher to be received on trial?

Answ. 1. By the Annual Conference.

2. In the interval of the Conference, by a Bishop, or the Presiding Elder of the district, until the sitting of the Conference.

But no one shall be received unless he first procure a recommendation from the Quarterly Conference of his circuit or station. We may then, if he give us satisfaction, receive him on trial. And before any such candidate is received into full connexion, or ordained Deacon or Elder, he shall give satisfactory evidence respecting his knowledge of those particular subjects which have been recommended to his consideration.

When a preacher's name is not printed in the Minutes, he must receive a written license from a Bishop, or Presiding Elder.

Observe! taking on trial is entirely different from admitting a preacher into full connexion. One on trial may be either admitted, or rejected without doing him any wrong:—otherwise it would be no trial at all.

At each Annual Conference, those who are received on trial, or are admitted into full connexion, shall be asked whether they are willing to devote themselves to the missionary work; and a list of the names of all those who are willing to do so shall be taken and reported to the Corresponding Secretary of the Missionary Society; and all such shall be considered as ready and willing to be employed as missionaries whenever called for by either of the Bishops.

SECTION VIII.

Of Receiving Travelling Preachers into Full Connexion.

Quest. What method do we use in receiving a preacher at the Conference into full connexion?

Answ. After solemn fasting and prayer, every person proposed shall then be asked, before the Conference, the following questions, (with any others which may be thought necessary,) namely :—Have you faith in Christ? Are you going on to perfection? Do you expect to be made perfect in love in this life? Are you groaning after it? Are you resolved to devote yourself wholly to God and his work? Do you know the rules of society?—of the bands? Do you keep them? Do you constantly attend the sacrament? Have you read the form of Discipline? Are you willing to conform to it? Have you considered the rules of a preacher, (see § 9,) especially the first, tenth, and twelfth? Will you keep them for conscience' sake? Are you determined to employ all your time in the work of God? Will you endeavour not to speak too long or too loud? Will you diligently instruct the children in every place? Will you visit from house to house? Will you recommend fasting, or abstinence, both by precept and example? Are you in debt?

Then if he give us satisfaction, after he has been employed two successive years in the regular itinerant work on circuits or in stations, which is to commence from his being received on trial at the Annual Conference, and being approved by the Annual Conference, and examined by the President of the Conference, he may be received into full connexion.

N. B. A Missionary employed on a Foreign Mission may be admitted into full connexion, if recommended by the Superintendent of the Mission where he labours, without being present at the Annual Conference for examination.

SECTION IX.

Of the Rules for a Preacher's Conduct.

Quest. 1. What are the directions given to a Preacher?

Answ. 1. Be diligent. Never be unemployed: never be triflingly employed. Never trifle away time: neither spend any more time at any place than is strictly necessary.

2. Be serious. Let your motto be, *Holiness to the Lord.* Avoid all lightness, jesting, and foolish talking.

3. Converse sparingly, and conduct yourself prudently with women. 1 Tim. v, 2.

4. Take no step toward marriage without first consulting with your brethren.

5. Believe evil of no one without good evidence; unless you see it done, take heed how you credit it. Put the best construction on everything. You know the judge is always supposed to be on the prisoner's side.

6. Speak evil of no one; because your word, especially, would eat as doth a canker. Keep your thoughts within your own breast, till you come to the person concerned

7. Tell every one under your care what you think wrong in his conduct and temper, and that lovingly and plainly as sóon as may be: else it will fester in your heart. Make all haste to cast the fire out of your bosom.

8. Avoid all affectation. A preacher of the gospel is the servant of all.

9. Be ashamed of nothing but sin.

10. Be punctual. Do everything exactly at the time. And do not mend our rules, but keep them; not for wrath but conscience' sake.

11. You have nothing to do but to save souls: therefore spend and be spent in this work; and go always not only to those that want you, but to those that want you most.

Observe! it is not your business only to preach so many times, and to take care of this or that society; but to save as many as you can; to bring as many sinners as you can to repentance, and with all your power to build them up in that holiness without which they cannot see the Lord. And remember!—a Methodist Preacher is to mind every point, great and small, in the Methodist Discipline! Therefore you will need to exercise all the sense and grace you have.

12. Act in all things not according to your own will, but as a son in the gospel. As such, it is your duty to employ your time in the manner in which we direct: in preaching, and visiting from house to house; in reading, meditation, and prayer. Above all, if you labour with us in the Lord's vineyard, it is needful you should do that part of the work which we advise, at those times and places which we judge most for his glory.

Quest. 2. Are there any smaller advices which might be of use to us?

Answ. Perhaps these: 1. Be sure never

to disappoint a congregation. 2. Begin at the time appointed. 3. Let your whole deportment be serious, weighty, and solemn. 4. Always suit your subject to your audience. 5. Choose the plainest texts you can. 6. Take care not to ramble, but keep to your text, and make out what you take in hand. 7. Take care of anything awkward or affected, either in your gesture, phrase, or pronunciation. 8. Do not usually pray, *extempore*, above eight or ten minutes (at most) without intermission. 9. Frequently read and enlarge upon a portion of Scripture; and let young preachers often exhort without taking a text. 10. Always avail yourself of the great festivals, by preaching on the occasion.

SECTION X.

Of the Duty of Preachers to God, themselves, and one another.

Quest. 1. What is the duty of a preacher?

Answ. 1. To preach.

2. To meet the societies, classes, and general bands.

3. To visit the sick.

4. To preach in the morning where he can get hearers. We recommend morning preaching at five o'clock in the summer, and six in the winter, wherever it is practicable.

Quest. 2. How shall a preacher be qualified for his charge?

Answ. By walking closely with God, and having his work greatly at heart: and by understanding and loving discipline, ours in particular.

Quest. 3. Do we sufficiently watch over each other?

Answ. We do not. Should we not frequently ask each other, Do you walk closely with God? Have you now fellowship with the Father and the Son? At what hour do you rise? Do you punctually observe the morning and evening hours of retirement? Do you spend the day in the manner which the Conference advises? Do you converse seriously, usefully, and closely? To be more particular: Do you use all the means of grace yourself, and enforce the use of them on all other persons? They are either instituted or prudential.

I. The instituted are,

1. Prayer: private, family, and public; consisting of deprecation, petition, intercession, and thanksgiving. Do you use each of these? Do you forecast daily, wherever you are, to secure time for private devotion? Do you practise it everywhere? Do you ask everywhere, Have you family prayer? Do you ask individuals, Do you use private prayer every morning and evening in particular?

2. Searching the Scriptures, by

(1) Reading: constantly, some part of every day; regularly, all the Bible in order; carefully, with notes; seriously, with prayer before and after; fruitfully, immediately practising what you learn there?

(2) Meditating: At set times? By rule?

(3) Hearing: Every opportunity? With prayer before, at, after? Have you a Bible always about you?

3. The Lord's supper: Do you use this at every opportunity? With solemn prayer before? With earnest and deliberate self-devotion?

4. Fasting: Do you use as much abstinence and fasting every week, as your health, strength, and labour will permit?

5. Christian conference: Are you convinced how important and how difficult it is to order your conversation aright? Is it always in grace? Seasoned with salt? Meet to minister grace to the hearers? Do you not converse too long at a time? Is not an hour commonly enough? Would it not be well always to have a determined end in view? And to pray before and after it?

II. Prudential means we may use either as Christians, as Methodists, or as preachers.

1. As Christians: What particular rules have you in order to grow in grace? What arts of holy living?

2. As Methodists: Do you never miss your class or band?

3. As Preachers: Have you thoroughly considered your duty? And do you make a conscience of executing every part of it? Do you meet every society? Also, the leaders and bands?

These means may be used without fruit. But there are some means which cannot; namely, watching, denying ourselves, taking up our cross, exercise of the presence of God.

1. Do you steadily watch against the world? Yourself? Your besetting sin?

2. Do you deny yourself every useless pleasure of sense? Imagination? Honour? Are you temperate in all things? Instance in food: (1) Do you use only that kind and that degree which is best both for body and soul? Do you see the necessity of this? (2) Do you eat no more at each meal than is necessary? Are you not heavy or drowsy after dinner? (3) Do you use only that kind, and that degree of drink, which is best both for your body and soul? (4) Do you choose and use water for your common drink? And only take wine medicinally or sacramentally?

3. Wherein do you take up your cross daily? Do you cheerfully bear your cross, however grievous to nature, as a gift of God, and labour to profit thereby?

4. Do you endeavour to set God always before you? To see his eye continually fixed upon you? Never can you use these means but a blessing will ensue. And the more you use them, the more you will grow in grace.

SECTION XI.

Of the Duties of those who have the Charge of Circuits or Stations.

Quest. 1. What are the duties of the Elder, Deacon, or preacher, who has the special charge of a circuit?

Answ. 1. To see that the other preachers in his circuit behave well, and want nothing.

2. To renew the tickets for the admission of members into love-feast quarterly, and regulate the bands.

3. To meet the Stewards and Leaders as often as possible.

4. To appoint all the Leaders, to change them when he sees it necessary, and to examine each of them, with all possible exactness, at least once a quarter, concerning his method of meeting a class. (See part i, ch. v, § 3, page 79.)

5. To receive, try, and expel members, according to the form of Discipline.

6. To hold watch-nights and love-feasts.

7. To hold quarterly meetings in the absence of the Presiding Elder.

8. To take care that every society be duly supplied with books.

9. To take an exact account of the members in society, and of the probationers, in their respective circuits and stations, keeping the names of all local Elders, Deacons, and preachers, properly distinguished, and deliver in such account to the Annual Conference, that their number may be printed in the Minutes.

10. To give an account of his circuit every quarter to his Presiding Elder.

11. To meet the men and women apart, in the large societies, once a quarter, wherever it is practicable.

12. To examine the accounts of all the Stewards.

13. To appoint a person to receive the quarterly collection in the *classes.*

14. To see that *public* collections be made quarterly, if need be.

15. To encourage the support of missions (see part iii, ch. iv) and Sunday schools, and the publication and distribution of Bibles, tracts, (see part iii, ch. vi,) and Sunday-school books, by forming societies and making collections for these objects in such way and manner as the Annual Conference to which he belongs, shall from time to time direct.

16. To publicly catechise the children in the Sunday school and at special meetings appointed for that purpose. It shall also be the duty of each preacher, in connexion with reporting the Sunday-school statistics at each Quarterly Conference, to state to what extent he has publicly or privately catechised the children of his charge.

17. To form Bible classes for the larger children and youth, and to attend to all the duties prescribed for the training of children in part i, ch. vi, page 85.

18. If the Annual Conference to which he belongs should not give any directions on the subject, to take up a collection in the course of the year, or raise a subscription, as he may judge expedient, the proceeds of which shall be at his disposal in the purchase and distribution of tracts.

19. To lay before the Quarterly Conference, at each quarterly meeting, as far as practicable, to be entered on its journal, a written statement of the number and state of the Sunday schools in the circuit or sta-

tion, and to report the same to his Annual Conference according to the form published by the Sunday-School Union of the Methodist Episcopal Church, together with the amount raised for the support of missions, and for the publication of Bibles and tracts.

20. To take an annual collection in each of his appointments in behalf of the Sunday-School Union.

21. To raise a yearly subscription in those circuits that can bear it, for building churches, and paying the debts of those which have been already erected.

22. To choose a committee of lay members to make a just application of the money where it is most wanted.

Quest. 2. What other directions shall we give him?

Answ. Several.

1. To take a regular catalogue of the societies in towns and cities, as they live in the streets.

2. To leave his successor a particular account of the circuit, including an account of the subscribers for our periodicals.

3. To see that every band-leader have the rules of the bands.

4. To enforce vigorously, but calmly, all the rules of the society.

5. As soon as there are four men or women believers in any place, to put them into a band.

6. To suffer no love-feast to last above an hour and a half.

7 To warn all from time to time, that

none are to remove from one circuit to another, without a note of recommendation from the preacher of the circuit in these words:—"*A. B., the bearer, has been an acceptable member of the Methodist Episcopal Church.*" And to inform them that, without such a certificate, they will not be received into the Church in other places.

8. To recommend everywhere decency and cleanliness.

9. To read the rules of the society, with the aid of the other preachers, once a year in every congregation, and once a quarter in every society.

10. The preacher who has the charge of a circuit shall appoint prayer meetings wherever he can in his circuit.

11. Wherever it is practicable, he shall so arrange the appointments as to give the local preachers regular and systematic employment on the Sabbath.

12. He shall take care that a fast be held in every society in his circuit, on the Friday preceding every quarterly meeting: and that a memorandum of it be written on all the class papers.

13. To license such persons as he may judge proper to officiate as exhorters in the Church, provided no person shall be so licensed without the consent of the leaders' meeting, or of the class of which he is a member, where no leaders' meeting is held; and the exhorters so authorized shall be subject to the annual examination of character in the Quarterly Conference, and have their

license annually renewed by the Presiding Elder, or the preacher having the charge, if approved by the Quarterly Conference.

N. B. The preachers who have the oversight of circuits are required to execute all our rules fully and strenuously against all frauds, and particularly against dishonest insolvencies; suffering none to remain in our Church on any account who are found guilty of any fraud.

☞ For the mode of procedure in case of insolvency of members, and in settling disputes, &c., as to the payment of debts or otherwise, see part i, chapter ix, section 4, quest. 2, 3, pages 100–102.

Quest. 3. What can be done to supply the circuits during the sittings of the Conferences?

Answ. 1. Let all the appointments stand according to the plan of the circuit.

2. Engage as many local preachers and exhorters as will supply them; and let them be paid for their time in proportion to the allowance of the travelling preachers.

3. If preachers and exhorters cannot attend, let some person of ability be appointed in every society, to sing, pray, and read one of Mr. Wesley's sermons.

4. But if that cannot be done, let there be prayer meetings.

SECTION XII.

Of the Matter and Manner of Preaching.

Quest. 1. What is the best general method of preaching?

Answ. 1. To convince: 2. To offer Christ: 3. To invite: 4. To build up: And to do this in some measure in every sermon.

Quest. 2. What is the most effectual way of preaching Christ?

Answ. The most effectual way of preaching Christ is, to preach him in all his offices; and to declare his law, as well as his gospel, both to believers and unbelievers. Let us strongly and closely insist upon inward and outward holiness in all its branches.

SECTION XIII.

Rules by which we should continue, or desist from, Preaching at any Place.

Quest. 1. Is it advisable for us to preach in as many places as we can, without forming any societies?

Answ. By no means. We have made the trial in various places; and that for a considerable time. But all the seed has fallen by the way-side. There is scarce any fruit remaining.

Quest. 2. Where should we endeavour to preach most?

Answ. 1. Where there is the greatest number of quiet and willing hearers.

2. Where there is most fruit.

Quest. 3. Ought we not diligently to observe in what places God is pleased at any time to pour out his Spirit more abundantly?

Answ. We ought: and at that time to send more labourers than usual into that part of the harvest.

SECTION XIV.

Of Visiting from House to House, Guarding against those things that are so common to Professors, and Enforcing Practical Religion.

Quest. 1. How can we further assist those under our care?

Answ. By instructing them at their own houses. What unspeakable need is there of this! The world says, "*The Methodists are no better than other people.*" This is not true in the general: but, 1. Personal religion, either toward God or man, is too superficial among us. We can but just touch on a few particulars. How little faith is there among us! How little communion with God, how little living in heaven, walking in eternity, deadness to every creature! How much love of the world! Desire of pleasure, of ease, of getting money! How little brotherly love! What continual judging one another! What gossipping, evil-speaking, tale-bearing! What want of moral honesty! To instance only one particular;

who does as he would be done by in buying and selling?

2. Family religion is wanting in many branches. And what avails public preaching alone, though we could preach like angels? We must—yea, every travelling preacher must—instruct the people from house to house. Till this be done, and that in good earnest, Methodists will be no better.

Our religion is not sufficiently deep, universal, uniform; but superficial, partial, uneven. It will be so till we spend half as much time in this visiting, as we now do in talking uselessly. Can we find a better method of doing this than Mr. Baxter's? If not, let us adopt it without delay. His whole tract, entitled *Gildas Salvianus*, is well worth a careful perusal. Speaking of this visiting from house to house, he says, (p. 351,) "We shall find many hinderances, both in ourselves and the people."

1. In ourselves there is much dulness and laziness, so that there will be much ado to get us to be faithful in the work.

2. We have a base, man-pleasing temper, so that we let them perish rather than lose their love; we let them go quietly to hell, lest we should offend them.

3. Some of us have a foolish bashfulness. We know not how to begin, and blush to contradict the devil.

4. But the greater hinderance is weakness of faith. Our whole motion is weak, because the spring of it is weak.

5. Lastly, we are unskilful in the work. How few know how to deal with men, so as to get within them, and suit all our discourse to their several conditions and tempers: to choose the fittest subjects, and follow them with a holy mixture of seriousness, terror, love, and meekness!

But undoubtedly this private application is implied in those solemn words of the apostle: "I charge thee before God and the Lord Jesus Christ, who shall judge the quick and the dead at his appearing, preach the word: be instant in season, out of season: reprove, rebuke, exhort, with all long-suffering."

O, brethren, if we could but set this work on foot in all our societies, and prosecute it zealously, what glory would redound to God! If the common lukewarmness were banished, and every shop, and every house, busied in speaking of the word and works of God, surely God would dwell in our habitations, and make us his delight.

And this is absolutely necessary to the welfare of our people, some of whom neither repent nor believe to this day. Look round, and see how many of them are still in apparent danger of damnation. And how can you walk and talk, and be merry with such people, when you know their case? When you look them in the face, you should break forth into tears, as the prophet did when he looked upon Hazael, and then set on them with the most vehement exhortations. O, for God's sake, and the sake of poor souls, bestir yourselves, and spare no pains that may conduce to their salvation!

What cause have we to bleed before the Lord that we have so long neglected this good work! If we had but engaged in it sooner, how many more might have been brought to Christ! And how much holier and happier might our societies have been before now! And why might we not have done it sooner? There were many hinderances; and so there always will be. But the greatest hinderance is in ourselves—in our littleness of faith and love.

But it is objected, I. "This will take up so much time, we shall not have leisure to follow our studies." We answer, 1. Gaining knowledge is a good thing, but saving souls is a better. 2. By this very thing you will gain the most excellent knowledge—that of God and eternity. 3. You will have time for gaining other knowledge too. Only sleep no more than you need; "and never be idle, or triflingly employed." But, 4. If you can do but one, let your studies alone. We ought to throw by all the libraries in the world, rather than be guilty of the loss of one soul.

It is objected, II. "The people will not submit to it." If some will not, others will. And the success with them will repay all your labour. O let us herein follow the example of St. Paul! 1. For our general business, *Serving the Lord with all humility of mind:* 2. Our special work, *Take heed to yourselves, and to all the flock:* 3. Our doctrine, *Repentance toward God, and faith toward our Lord Jesus Christ:* 4. The place, *I have taught you publicly, and from house to house:* 5. The object and manner of teaching, *I ceased not to warn every one, night and day, with tears:* 6. His innocence and self-denial herein, *I have coveted no man's silver or gold:* 7. His patience, *Neither count I my life dear unto myself.* And among all other motives, let these be ever before our eyes: 1. *The Church of God, which he hath purchased with his own blood:* 2. *Grievous wolves shall enter in; yea, of yourselves shall men arise, speaking perverse things.*

Write this upon your hearts, and it will do you more good than twenty years' study. Then you will have no time to spare; you will have work enough. Then likewise no preacher will stay with us who is as salt that has lost its savour. For to such this employment would be mere drudgery. And in order to it, you will have need of all the knowledge you can procure, and grace you can attain.

The sum is, Go into every house in course, and teach every one therein, young and old, to be Christians inwardly and outwardly; make every particular plain to their understandings; fix it in their minds; write it on their hearts. In order to this there must be line upon line, precept upon precept. What patience, what love, what knowledge, is requisite for this! We must needs do this, were it only to avoid idleness.

Do we not loiter away many hours in every week? Each try himself: no idleness is consistent with a growth in grace. Nay, without exactness in redeeming time, you cannot retain the grace you receive in justification.

Quest. 2. Why are we not more holy? Why do we not live in eternity? Walk with God all the day long? Why are we not all devoted to God? Breathing the whole spirit of missionaries?

Answ. Chiefly because we are enthusiasts; looking for the end without using the means. To touch only upon two or three instances:—Who of us rises at four, or even at five, when we do not preach? Do we know the obligation and benefit of fasting or abstinence? How often do we practise it? The neglect of this alone is sufficient to account for our feebleness and faintness of spirit. We are continually grieving the Holy Spirit of God by the habitual neglect of a plain duty. Let us amend from this hour.

Quest. 3. How shall we guard against Sabbath-breaking, evil-speaking, unprofitable conversation, lightness, expensiveness or gayety of apparel, and contracting debts without due care to discharge them?

Answ. 1. Let us preach expressly on each of these heads. 2. Read in every society the sermon on evil-speaking. 3. Let the leaders closely examine and exhort every person to put away the accursed thing. 4. Let the preachers warn every society that none who is guilty herein can remain with us. 5. Extirpate buying or selling goods which have not paid the duty laid upon them by government out of our Church. Let none remain with us who will not totally abstain from this evil in every kind and degree. Extirpate bribery, receiving anything, directly or indirectly, for voting at any election. Show no respect to persons herein, but expel all that touch the accursed thing. And strongly advise our people to discountenance all treats given by candidates before or at elections, and not to be partakers, in any respect, of such iniquitous practices.

SECTION XV.

Of Employing our Time profitably, when we are not travelling, or engaged in Public Exercises.

Quest. 1. What general method of employing our time shall we advise?

Answ. We advise you, 1. As often as possible to rise at four. 2. From four to five in the morning, and from five to six in the evening, to meditate, pray, and read the Scriptures with notes, and the closely practical parts of what Mr. Wesley has published. 3. From six in the morning till twelve, (allowing an hour for breakfast,) read, with much prayer, some of our best religious tracts.

Quest. 2. Why is it that the people under our care are not better?

Answ. Other reasons may concur, but the chief is, because we are not more knowing and more holy.

Quest. 3. But why are we not more knowing?

Answ. Because we are idle. We forget our first rule, "Be diligent. Never be unemployed. Never be triflingly employed. Neither spend any more time at any place than is strictly necessary." We fear there is altogether a fault in this matter, and that few of us are clear. Which of us spend as many hours a day in God's work as we did formerly in man's work? We talk,—talk or read what comes next to hand. We must, absolutely must, cure this evil, or betray the cause of God. But how? 1. Read the most useful books, and that regularly and constantly. 2. Steadily spend all the morning in this employment, or at least five hours in the four and twenty. "But I have no taste for reading." Contract a taste for it by use, or return to your former employment. "But I have no books." Be diligent to spread the books, and you will have the use of them.

SECTION XVI.

Of the Necessity of Union among ourselves.

Let us be deeply sensible (from what we have known) of the evil of a division in principle, spirit, or practice, and the dreadful consequences to ourselves and others. If we are united, what can stand before us?

If we divide, we shall destroy ourselves, the work of God, and the souls of our people.

Quest. What can be done in order to a closer union with each other?

Answ. 1. Let us be deeply convinced of the absolute necessity of it.

2. Pray earnestly for, and speak freely to, each other.

3. When we meet, let us never part without prayer.

4. Take great care not to despise each other's gifts.

5. Never speak lightly of each other.

6. Let us defend each other's character in everything so far as is consistent with truth.

7. Labour in honour each to prefer the other before himself.

8. We recommend a serious perusal of *The Causes, Evils, and Cures of Heart and Church Divisions.*

SECTION XVII.

Of Supernumerary and Superannuated or Worn-out Preachers.

A supernumerary preacher is one so worn out in the itinerant service as to be rendered incapable of preaching constantly; but at the same time is willing to do any work in the ministry which the Conference may direct, and his strength enable him to perform.

A supernumerary preacher, who refuses to attend to the work assigned him, unless in case of sickness, or other unavoidable cause or causes, shall not be allowed to exercise the functions of his office, nor even to preach among us; *nevertheless*, the final determination of the case shall be with the Annual Conference of which he is a member, who shall have power to acquit, suspend, locate, or expel him, as the case may be.

Every superannuated preacher, who may reside without the bounds of the Conference of which he is a member, shall annually forward to his Conference a certificate of his Christian and ministerial conduct, together with an account of the number and circumstances of his family, signed by the Presiding Elder of the district, or the preacher in charge of the circuit or station within whose bounds he may reside; without which the Conference shall not be required to allow his claim.

SECTION XVIII.

Local Preachers.

Quest. What directions shall be given concerning local preachers?

Answ. 1. The Quarterly Conference shall have authority to license proper persons to preach, and renew their license annually, when, in the judgment of said Conference, their gifts, grace, and usefulness, will warrant such renewal; to recommend suitable candidates to the Annual Conference for Deacons' or Elders' orders in the local connexion, for admission on trial in the travelling connexion, and to try, suspend, expel, or acquit, any local preacher in the circuit or station against whom charges may be brought. *Provided*, that no person shall be licensed to preach without the recommendation of the society of which he is a member, or of a Leaders' meeting. Nor shall any one be licensed to preach, or recommended to the Annual Conference to travel, or for ordination, without first being examined in the Quarterly Conference on the subject of doctrines and discipline. (See part i, ch. iii, § 4, page 39.)

2. A licensed local preacher shall be eligible to the office of a Deacon, after he has preached four years from the time he received a regular license, and has obtained a testimonial from the Quarterly Conference, after proper examination, signed by the President, and countersigned by the Secretary; and after his character has passed in examination before, and he has obtained the approbation of, the Annual Conference.

3. A local Deacon shall be eligible to the office of an Elder, after he has preached four years from the time he was ordained a Deacon, and has obtained a recommendation from the Quarterly Conference of which he is a member, certifying his qualifications in doctrine, discipline, talents, and usefulness, signed by the President, and countersigned by the Secretary. He shall, if he cannot attend, send to the Annual Conference such recommendation, and a note certifying his belief in the doctrine and Discipline of our Church. The whole being examined by the Annual Conference, and

if approved he may be ordained: *provided*, nevertheless, no slaveholder shall be eligible to the office of an Elder or Deacon, where the laws will admit of emancipation, and permit the liberated slave to enjoy freedom.

4. Every local Elder, Deacon, or preacher, shall be amenable to the Quarterly Conference where he resides, for his Christian character and the faithful performance of his ministerial office. He shall have his name recorded on the journal of said Conference, and also enrolled on a class paper, and shall meet in class; and in neglect of the above duties, the Quarterly Conference, if they judge it proper, may deprive him of his ministerial office. And when a preacher is located, or discontinued by an Annual Conference, he shall be amenable to the Quarterly Conference of the circuit or station where he had his last appointment, or at the place where he shall reside at the time of his location.

Whenever any Elder, Deacon, or preacher, shall remove from one circuit or station to another, he shall procure from the Presiding Elder of the district, or from the preacher having charge, a certificate of his official standing in the Church at the time of his removal, without which he shall not be received as a local preacher in other places.

5. The Presiding Elders and the preachers in charge, are required so to arrange the appointments, wherever it is practicable, as to give the local preachers regular and systematic employment on the Sabbath.

CHAPTER V.

OF THE MEANS OF GRACE.

SECTION I.

Of Public Worship.

Quest. 1. WHAT directions shall be given for the establishment of uniformity in public worship among us, on the Lord's day?

Answ. 1. Let the morning service consist of singing, prayer, the reading of a chapter out of the Old Testament, and another out of the New, and preaching.

2. Let the afternoon service consist of singing, prayer, the reading of one or two chapters out of the Bible, and preaching.

3. Let the evening service consist of singing, prayer, and preaching.

4. But on the days of administering the Lord's supper, the two chapters in the morning service may be omitted.

5. In administering the ordinances, and in the burial of the dead, let the form of Discipline invariably be used. Let the Lord's prayer also be used on all occasions of public worship in concluding the first prayer, and the apostolic benediction in dismissing the congregation.

6. Let the society be met, wherever it is practicable, on the Sabbath-day.

Quest. 2. Is there not a great indecency sometimes practised among us, namely, talking in the congregation before and after service. How shall this be cured?

Answ. Let all the ministers and preachers join as one man, and enlarge on the impropriety of talking before or after service; and strongly exhort those that are concerned to do it no more. In three months, if we are in earnest, this vile practice will be banished out of every Methodist congregation. Let none stop till he has carried his point.

SECTION II.

Of the Spirit and Truth of Singing.

Quest. How shall we guard against formality in singing?

Answ. 1. By choosing such hymns as are proper for the congregation.

2. By not singing too much at once; seldom more than five or six verses.

3. By suiting the tune to the words.

4. By often stopping short, and asking the people, "Now! do you know what you said last? Did you speak no more than you felt?"

5. Do not suffer the people to sing too slow. This naturally tends to formality, and is brought in by those who have either very strong or very weak voices.

6. In every large society let them learn to sing; and let them always learn our tunes first.

7. Let the women constantly sing their parts alone. Let no man sing with them unless he understands the notes, and sings the base as it is composed in the tune-book.

8. Introduce no new tune till they are perfect in the old.

9. Recommend our tune-book. And if you cannot sing yourself, choose a person or two at each place to pitch the tune for you.

10. Exhort every person in the congregation to sing; not one in ten only.

11. Sing no hymns of your own composing.

12. If a preacher be present, let him alone give out the words.

13. When the singers would teach a tune to the congregation, they must sing only the tenor, [the air.]

14. Let it be recommended to our people not to attend the singing schools which are not under our direction.

15. The preachers are desired not to encourage the singing of fugue tunes in our congregations.

16. We do not think that fugue tunes are sinful or improper to be used in private companies; but we do not approve of their being used in our public congregations, because public singing is a part of divine worship in which all the congregation ought to join

SECTION III.

Of Class-meetings and Love-feasts.

Quest. 1. How may the Leaders of classes be rendered more useful?

Answ. 1. Let each of them be diligently examined concerning his method of meeting a class. Let this be done with all possible exactness, at least once a quarter. In order to this, take sufficient time.

2. Let each Leader carefully inquire how every soul of his class prospers: not only how each person observes the outward rules, but how he grows in the knowledge and love of God.

3. Let the Leaders converse with those who have the charge of their circuits, frequently and freely.

Quest. 2. Can anything more be done in order to make the Class-meetings lively and profitable?

Answ. 1. Change improper Leaders.

2. Let the Leaders frequently meet each other's classes.

3. Let us observe which Leaders are the most useful; and let these meet the other classes as often as possible.

4. See that all the Leaders be not only men of sound judgment, but men truly devoted to God.

Quest. 3. What shall we do with those members of our Church who wilfully and repeatedly neglect to meet their class?

Answ. 1. Let the Elder, Deacon, or one of the preachers, visit them, whenever it is practicable, and explain to them the consequence if they continue to neglect, namely, exclusion.

2. If they do not amend, let him who has the charge of the circuit or station bring their case before the society, or a select number, before whom they shall have been

cited to appear; and if they be found guilty of wilful neglect by a decision of a majority of the members before whom their case is brought, let them be laid aside, and let the preacher show that they are excluded for a breach of our rules, and not for immoral conduct.

Quest. 4. How often shall we permit serious persons who are not of our Church to meet in class?

Answ. At every other meeting of the class in every place let no stranger be admitted. At other times they may; but the same person not above twice or thrice.

Quest. 5. How often shall we permit strangers to be present at our Love-feasts?

Answ. Let them be admitted with the utmost caution; and the same person on no account above twice or thrice, unless he become a member.

SECTION IV.

Of the Band Societies.

Two, three, or four true believers, who have confidence in each other, form a band. Only it is to be observed, that in one of these bands all must be men, or all women; and all married, or all unmarried.

[*Rules of the Band Societies, drawn up Dec.* 25, 1738.]

The design of our meeting is to obey that command of God, *Confess your faults one to another, and pray one for another, that ye may be healed.* James v, 16.

To this end we agree,

1. To meet once a week at least.

2. To come punctually at the hour appointed, without some extraordinary reason prevents.

3. To begin exactly at the hour with singing or prayer.

4. To speak, each of us in order, freely and plainly, the true state of our souls, with the faults we have committed in tempers, words, or actions, and the temptations we have felt, since our last meeting.

5. To end every meeting with prayer suited to the state of each person present.

6. To desire some person among us to speak his own state first, and then to ask the rest in order as many and as searching questions as may be, concerning their state, sins, and temptations.

Some of the questions proposed to one before he is admitted among us may be to this effect:

1. Have you the forgiveness of your sins?

2. Have you peace with God, through our Lord Jesus Christ?

3. Have you the witness of God's Spirit with your spirit, that you are a child of God?

4. Is the love of God shed abroad in your heart?

5. Has no sin, inward or outward, dominion over you?

6. Do you desire to be told of your faults?

7. Do you desire to be told of *all* your faults, and that plain and home?

8. Do you desire that every one of us should tell you, from time to time, whatsoever is in our heart concerning you?

9. Consider! Do you desire we should tell you whatsoever we think, whatsoever we fear, whatsoever we hear, concerning you?

10. Do you desire that in doing this, we should come as close as possible, that we should cut to the quick, and search your heart to the bottom?

11. Is it your desire and design to be on this and all other occasions entirely open, so as to speak without disguise, and without reserve?

Any of the preceding questions may be asked as often as occasion requires; the four following at every meeting:

1. What known sins have you committed since our last meeting?

2. What particular temptations have you met with?

3. How were you delivered?

4. What have you thought, said, or done, of which you doubt whether it be sin or not?

Directions given to the Band Societies, December 25, 1744.

You are supposed to have the *faith that overcometh the world.* To you, therefore, it is not grievous:

I. Carefully to abstain from doing evil: in particular,

1. Neither to *buy* nor *sell* anything at all on the Lord's day.

2. To taste no spirituous liquor, no dram of any kind, unless prescribed by a physician.

3. To be *at a word* both in buying and selling.

4. Not to *mention the faults* of any *behind his back*, and to stop those short that do.

5. To wear no *needless ornaments*, such as rings, ear-rings, necklaces, lace, or ruffles.

6. *To use* no *needless self-indulgence.*

II. Zealously to maintain good works: in particular,

1. To *give alms* of such things as you possess, and that according to your ability.

2. To reprove those who sin in your sight, and that in love and meekness of wisdom.

3. To be patterns of *diligence* and *frugality*, of *self-denial*, and taking up the cross daily.

III. Constantly to attend on all the ordinances of God: in particular,

1. To be at church, and at the LORD'S table, and at every public meeting of the bands, at every opportunity.

2. To use private prayer every day; and family prayer, if you are the head of a family.

3. Frequently to read the Scriptures, and meditate thereon. And,

4. To observe, as days of fasting, or abstinence, all *Fridays in the year.*

CHAPTER VI.

OF SUNDAY SCHOOLS AND THE RELIGIOUS INSTRUCTION OF CHILDREN.

Quest. WHAT shall we do for the rising generation?

Answ. 1. Let Sunday schools be formed in all our congregations where ten children can be collected for that purpose. And it shall be the special duty of preachers having charge of circuits and stations, with the aid of the other preachers, to see that this be done; to engage the co-operation of as many of our members as they can; to visit the schools as often as practicable; to preach on the subject of Sunday schools and religious instruction in each congregation at least once in six months; to lay before the Quarterly Conference at each quarterly meeting, to be entered on its journal, a written statement of the number and state of the Sunday schools within their respective circuits and stations, and to make a report of the same to their several Annual Conferences. Each Quarterly Conference shall have supervision of all the Sunday schools and Sunday-school societies within its bounds, which schools and societies shall be auxiliary to the Sunday-School Union of the Methodist Episcopal Church; and each Annual Conference shall report to said Union the number of auxiliaries within its bounds, together with other facts presented in the annual reports of the preachers as above directed.

2. It is recommended that each Annual Conference, where the general state of the work will allow, request the appointment of a special agent, to travel throughout its bounds, for the purpose of promoting the interests of Sunday schools; and his expenses shall be paid out of collections which he shall be directed to make, or otherwise, as shall be ordered by the Conference.

3. Let our catechisms be used as extensively as possible, both in our Sunday schools and families; and let the preachers faithfully enforce upon parents and Sunday-school teachers the great importance of instructing children in the doctrines and duties of our holy religion. Let the preachers also publicly catechise the children in the Sunday school, and at special meetings appointed for that purpose. It shall also be the duty of each preacher in connexion with reporting the Sabbath-school statistics at each Quarterly Conference, to state to what extent he has publicly or privately catechised the children of his charge.

4. It shall be the special duty of the preachers to form Bible classes wherever they can, for the instruction of larger children and youth; and where they cannot superintend them personally, to appoint suitable leaders for that purpose.

5. It shall be the duty of every preacher of a circuit or station to obtain the names of the children belonging to his congregations,

and leave a list of such names for his successor; and in his pastoral visits he shall pay special attention to the children, speak to them personally, and kindly, on experimental and practical godliness, according to their capacity, pray earnestly for them, and diligently instruct and exhort all parents to dedicate their children to the Lord in baptism as early as convenient; and let all baptized children be faithfully instructed in the nature, design, privileges, and obligations, of their baptism. Those of them who are well disposed may be admitted to our class-meetings and love-feasts; and such as are truly serious, and manifest a desire to flee the wrath to come, shall be advised to join society as probationers.

CHAPTER VII.

OF THE PRINTING AND CIRCULATION OF RELIGIOUS TRACTS.

Provision is made for the publication at the Book Concern of cheap books and tracts, in our own and foreign languages. For the duties of the Editor of tracts and Corresponding Secretary of the Tract Society, see part iii, ch. vi, art. 3, page 198. Our Tract Society is designed to aid in the diffusion of religious knowledge by the circulation of our evangelical publications.

1. It is recommended to our people everywhere to form Tract Societies, auxiliary to the Tract Society of the Methodist Episcopal Church.

2. It is recommended to preachers in charge, to make annually in their several congregations, collections in behalf of the Tract Society of the Methodist Episcopal Church.

CHAPTER VIII.

OF DRESS AND MARRIAGE.

SECTION I.

Of Dress.

Quest. SHOULD we insist on the rules concerning dress?

Answ. By all means. This is no time to give encouragement to superfluity of apparel. Therefore receive none into the Church till they have left off superfluous ornaments. In order to this, 1. Let every one who has charge of a circuit or station read Mr. Wesley's Thoughts upon Dress, at least once a year in every society. 2. In visiting the classes be very mild, but very strict. 3. Allow of no exempt case: better one suffer than many. 4. Give no tickets to any that wear high heads, enormous bonnets, ruffles, or rings.

SECTION II.

Of Marriage.

Quest. 1. Do we observe any evil which has prevailed in our Church with respect to marriage?

Answ. Many of our members have married with *unawakened* persons. This has produced bad effects; they have been either hindered for life, or have turned back to perdition.

Quest. 2. What can be done to discourage this?

Answ. 1. Let every preacher publicly enforce the apostle's caution, "Be ye not unequally yoked together with unbelievers." 2 Cor. vi, 14.

2. Let all be exhorted to take no step in so weighty a matter, without advising with the most serious of their brethren.

Quest. 3. Ought any woman to marry without the consent of her parents?

Answ. In general she ought not. Yet there may be exceptions. For if, 1. A woman believe it to be her duty to marry: if, 2. Her parents absolutely refuse to let her marry any Christian: then she may, nay, ought to marry without their consent. Yet even then a Methodist preacher ought not to be married to her.

We do not prohibit our people from marrying persons who are not of our Church, provided such persons have the form, and are seeking the power, of godliness; but we are determined to discourage their marrying persons who do not come up to this description.

CHAPTER IX.

OF BRINGING MINISTERS AND MEMBERS TO TRIAL, AND OF INSOLVENCIES, AND THE SETTLEMENT OF DISPUTES.

SECTION I.

Of the Trial of a Bishop.

Quest. 1. To whom is a Bishop amenable for his conduct?

Answ. To the General Conference, who have power to expel him for improper conduct, if they see it necessary.

Quest. 2. What provision shall be made for the trial of a Bishop, if he should be accused of immorality in the interval of the General Conference?

Answ. If a Bishop be accused of immorality, three Travelling Elders shall call upon him, and examine him on the subject; and if the three Elders verily believe that the Bishop is guilty of the crime, they shall call to their aid two Presiding Elders from two districts in the neighbourhood of that where the crime was committed, each of which Presiding Elders shall bring with him two Elders, or an Elder and a Deacon. The above-mentioned nine persons shall form a Conference, to examine into the charge brought against the Bishop: and if two-thirds of them verily believe him to be guilty of the crime laid to his charge, they shall have authority to suspend the Bishop till the ensuing General Conference, and the districts shall be regulated in the mean time as is provided in ch. iii, § 3, and ch. iv, §§ 1, 2; but no accusation shall be received against a Bishop except it be delivered in writing, signed by those who are to prove the crime; and a copy of the accusation shall be given to the accused Bishop.

SECTION II.

Of the Method of Proceeding against accused Travelling Ministers or Preachers.

Quest. 1. What shall be done when an Elder, Deacon, or preacher, is under report of being guilty of *some crime* expressly forbidden in the word of God, as an unchristian practice, sufficient to exclude a person from the kingdom of grace and glory?

Answ. 1. In the interval of the Annual Conference, let the Presiding Elder, in the absence of a Bishop, call as many travelling ministers as he shall think fit, at least three: and, if possible, bring the accused and the accuser face to face: and cause a correct record of the investigation to be kept and transmitted to the Annual Conference. If the person be clearly convicted, he shall be suspended from all ministerial services and Church privileges until the ensuing Annual Conference, at which his case shall be fully considered and determined. But if the accused be a *Presiding* Elder, the preachers must call in the Presiding Elder of the neighbouring district, who is required to attend and preside at the trial.

If the accused and accuser cannot be brought face to face, but the supposed delinquent flees from trial, it shall be received as a presumptive proof of guilt; and out of the mouth of two or three witnesses he shall be condemned. Nevertheless, even in that case, the Annual Conference shall reconsider and determine the whole matter.

And if the accused be a superannuated preacher, living out of the bounds of the Conference of which he is a member, he shall be held responsible to the Annual Conference within whose bounds he may reside, who shall have power to try, acquit, suspend, locate, or expel him, in the same manner as if he were a member of said Conference.

2. If the charge be preferred at the Conference, the case may be referred to a committee, in the presence of a Presiding Elder, or a member appointed by the Bishop in his stead, who shall cause a faithful record of the proceedings and testimony to be laid before the Conference; on which, with such other evidence as may be admitted, the case shall be decided.

Quest. 2. What shall be done in cases of improper tempers, words, or actions.

Answ. The person so offending shall be reprehended by his senior in office. Should a second transgression take place, one, two, or three ministers or preachers, are to be taken as witnesses. If he be not then cured, he shall be tried at the next Annual Conference, and, if found guilty and impenitent, shall be expelled from the connexion, and his name so returned in the Minutes of the Conference.

Quest. 3. What shall be done when a member of an Annual Conference fails in business, or contracts debts which he is not able to pay?

Answ. Let the Presiding Elder appoint three judicious members of the Church to inspect the accounts, contracts, and circumstances of the supposed delinquent, and if, in their opinion, he has behaved dishonestly, or contracted debts without the probability of paying, let the case be disposed of according to the answer of question one of this section.

Quest. 4. What shall be done with those ministers or preachers who hold and disseminate, publicly or privately, doctrines which are contrary to our articles of religion?

Answ. Let the same process be observed as in case of gross immorality: but if the minister or preacher so offending do solemnly engage not to disseminate such erroneous doctrines in public or in private, he shall be borne with, till his case be laid before the next Annual Conference, which shall determine the matter

Quest. 5. What shall be done when a travelling minister is accused of being so unacceptable, inefficient, or secular, as to be no longer useful in his work?

Answ. The Conference shall investigate the case, and if it appear that the complaint is well founded, and the accused will not voluntarily retire, the Conference may locate him without his consent.

Provided, nevertheless, that in all the above-mentioned cases of trial and conviction, an appeal to the ensuing General Conference shall be allowed, if the condemned person signify his intention to appeal, at the time of his condemnation, or at any time thereafter when he is informed thereof.

In all the above-mentioned cases it shall be the duty of the secretary of the Annual Conference carefully to preserve the minutes of the trial, whether taken before a committee or before the Conference, and all the documents relating to the case, together with the charge or charges, and the specification or specifications; which minutes and documents only, in case of an appeal from the decision of an Annual Conference, shall be presented to the General Conference, in evidence on the case. And in all cases, when an appeal is made, and admitted by the General Conference, the appellant shall either state personally, or by his representative, (who shall be a member of the Conference,) the grounds of his appeal, showing cause why he appeals, and he shall be allowed to make his defence without interruption. After which, the representatives of the Annual Conference from whose decision the appeal is made, shall be permitted to respond in presence of the appellant, who shall have the privilege of replying to such representatives, which shall close the pleadings on both sides. This done, the appellant shall withdraw, and the Conference shall decide. And after such form of trial and expulsion, the person so expelled shall have no privileges of society or sacraments in our Church, without confession, contrition, and satisfactory reformation.

A preacher on trial who may be accused of crime shall be accountable to the Quarterly Conference of the circuit on which he travels. The Presiding Elder shall call a committee of three local preachers, who may suspend him; and the Quarterly Conference may expel him: *nevertheless*, he shall have a right to an appeal to the next Annual Conference.

When any travelling elder or deacon is deprived of his credentials, by expulsion or otherwise, they shall be filed with the papers of the Annual Conference of which he was a member; and should he at any future time give satisfactory evidence to said Conference of his amendment, and procure a certificate of the Quarterly Conference of the circuit or station where he resides, or of an Annual Conference who may have admitted him on trial, recommending to the Annual Conference of which he *was* a member formerly the restoration of his credentials, the said Conference may restore them.

SECTION III.

Of the Trial of Local Preachers.

Quest. 1. What shall be done when a local Elder, Deacon, or preacher, is reported to be guilty of some crime expressly forbidden in the word of God, sufficient to exclude a person from the kingdom of grace and glory ?

Answ. 1. The preacher having charge shall call a committee, consisting of three or more local preachers, before whom it shall be the duty of the accused to appear, and by whom he shall be acquitted, or, if found guilty, suspended until the next Quarterly Conference. And the preacher in charge shall cause exact minutes of the charges, testimony, and examination, together with the decision of the committee, to be laid before the Quarterly Conference, where it shall be the duty of the accused to appear. If the accused refuse or neglect to appear before said committee, he may be tried in his absence.

And the president shall, at the commencement of the trial, appoint a secretary, who shall take down regular minutes of the evidence of the trial; which minutes, when read and approved, shall be signed by the president, and also by the members of the Conference who are present, or a majority of them. And in case of condemnation, the local preacher, Deacon, or Elder, shall be allowed to appeal to the next Annual Conference, provided that he signify to the said Quarterly Conference his determination to appeal; in which case the said president shall lay the minutes of the trial above mentioned before the said Annual Conference, at which the local preacher, Deacon, or Elder, so appealing, may appear: and the said Annual Conference shall judge, and finally determine, from the minutes of the said trial, so laid before them.

2. When a local Elder, or Deacon, shall be expelled, the Presiding Elder shall require of him the credentials of his ordination, to be filed with the papers of the Annual Conference within the limits of which the expulsion has taken place. And should he, at any future time, produce to the Annual Conference a certificate of his restoration, signed by the president, and countersigned by the secretary, of the Quarterly Conference, his credentials may be restored to him.

Quest. 2. What shall be done in cases of improper tempers, words, or actions?

Answ. The person so offending shall be reprehended by the preacher having charge. Should a second transgression take place, one, two, or three faithful friends, are to be taken as witnesses. If he be not then cured, he shall be tried at the next Quarterly Conference, and if found guilty and impenitent, he shall be expelled from the Church.

Quest. 3. What shall be done when a local Elder, Deacon, or preacher, fails in business, or contracts debts which he is not able to pay?

Answ. Let the preacher in charge appoint three judicious members of the Church to inspect the accounts, contracts, and circumstances, of the supposed delinquent; and if in their opinion he has behaved dishonestly, or contracted debts without the probability of paying, let the case be disposed of according to the answer to question one of this section.

SECTION IV.

Of bringing to Trial, finding guilty, and reproving, suspending, or excluding, Disorderly Persons from Society and Church Privileges, and of Insolvencies, and the settlement of Disputes.

Quest. 1. How shall an accused member be brought to trial?

Answ. 1. Before the society of which he is a member, or a select number of them, in the presence of a Bishop, Elder, Deacon, or preacher, in the following manner:—Let the accused and accuser be brought face to face; but if this cannot be done, let the next best evidence be procured. If the accused person be found guilty by the decision of a majority of the members before whom he is brought to trial, and the crime be such as is expressly forbidden by the word of God, sufficient to exclude a person from the kingdom of grace and glory, let the minister or preacher who has the charge of the circuit expel him. If the accused person evade a trial, by absenting himself, after sufficient notice given him, and the circumstances of the accusation afford strong presumption of guilt, let him be esteemed as guilty, and be accordingly excluded. Witnesses from without shall not be rejected.

2. But in cases of neglect of duties of any kind, imprudent conduct, indulging sinful tempers, or words, the buying, selling, or using, intoxicating liquors as a beverage, or disobedience to the order and discipline of the Church: (see part i, ch. v, § 3, quest. 3, page 80:) First, let private reproof be given by a preacher or leader; and if there be an acknowledgment of the fault, and proper humiliation, the person may be borne with. On a second offence, the preacher or leader may take one or two faithful friends. On a third offence, let the case be brought before the society, or a select number; and if there be no sign of real humiliation, the offender must be cut off.

3. If a member of our Church shall be clearly convicted of endeavouring to sow dissensions in any of our societies, by inveighing against either our doctrines or discipline, such person so offending shall be first reproved by the senior minister or preacher of his circuit, and if he persist in such pernicious practices, he shall be expelled from the Church.

4. *Nevertheless*, if in any of the abovementioned cases the minister or preacher differ in judgment from the majority of the ociety, or the select number, concerning

the innocence or guilt of the accused person, the trial, in such case, may be referred by the minister or preacher to the ensuing Quarterly Conference.

5. If there be a murmur or complaint from any excluded person, in any of the above-mentioned instances, that justice has not been done, he shall be allowed an appeal to the next Quarterly Conference: except such as absent themselves from trial, after sufficient notice is given them: and the majority of the Travelling and Local Preachers, Exhorters, Stewards, and Leaders present, shall finally determine the case.

After such forms of trial and expulsion, such person shall have no privileges of society or of sacraments in our Church, without contrition, confession, and satisfactory reformation.

Quest. 2. How shall disputes between members of our Church concerning the payment of debts or otherwise be settled?

Answ. 1. On any dispute between two or more of the members of our Church, concerning the payment of debts, or otherwise, which cannot be settled by the parties concerned, the preacher who has the charge of the circuit shall inquire into the circumstances of the case; and shall recommend to the contending parties a reference, consisting of one arbiter chosen by the plaintiff, and another chosen by the defendant; which two arbiters so chosen shall nominate the third; the three arbiters being members of our Church.

But if one of the parties be dissatisfied with the judgment given, such party may apply to the ensuing Quarterly Conference of the circuit, for allowance to have a *second* arbitration appointed; and if the Quarterly Conference see sufficient reason, they shall grant a *second* arbitration, in which case each party shall choose two arbiters, and the four arbiters shall choose a fifth, the judgment of the majority of whom shall be final: and any person refusing to abide by such judgment shall be excluded the Church.

And if any member of our Church shall refuse, in cases of debt or other disputes, to refer the matter to arbitration, when recommended by him who has the charge of the circuit, or shall enter into a lawsuit with another member before these measures are taken, he shall be expelled, unless the case be of such a nature as to require and justify a process at law.

2. Whenever a complaint is made against any member of our Church for non-payment of debt; when the accounts are adjusted, and the amount ascertained, the preacher having the charge shall call the debtor before a committee of at least three, to show cause why he does not make payment. The committee shall determine what further time shall be granted him for payment, and what security, if any, shall be given for payment; and in case the debtor refuses to comply, he shall be expelled; but in such case he may appeal to the Quarterly Con-

ference, and their decision shall be final. And in case the creditor complains that justice is not done him, he may lay his grievance before the Quarterly Conference, and their decision shall be final; and if the creditor refuse to comply, he shall be expelled.

Quest 3. What shall be done in case of insolvency on the part of any of our members?

Answ. 1. The preachers who have the oversight of circuits are required to execute all our rules fully and strenuously against all frauds, and particularly against dishonest insolvencies: suffering none to remain in our Church on any account who are found guilty of any fraud.

2. To prevent scandal, when any of our members fail in business, or contract debts which they are not able to pay, let two or three judicious members of the Church inspect the accounts, contracts, and circumstances of the case of the supposed delinquent; and if he have behaved dishonestly, or borrowed money without a probability of paying, let him be expelled.

PART II.

The Ritual.

CHAPTER I.

THE ORDER OF BAPTISM.

SECTION I.

General Directions.

1. LET every adult person, and the parents of every child to be baptized, have the choice either of immersion, sprinkling, or pouring.

2. We will on no account whatever make a charge for administering baptism, or for burying the dead.

SECTION II.

The Ministration of Baptism to Infants.

The minister coming to the font, which is to be filled with pure water, shall use the following.

Dearly beloved, forasmuch as all men are conceived and born in sin, and that our Saviour Christ saith, None can enter into the kingdom of God, except he be regenerate and born anew of water and of the Holy Ghost; I beseech you to call upon God the Father, through our Lord Jesus Christ, that of his bounteous mercy he will grant to *this child* that thing which by nature *he* cannot have, that *he* may be baptized with water and the Holy Ghost, and received into Christ's holy Church, and be made a *lively member* of the same.

Then shall the minister say,

Let us pray.

Almighty and everlasting God, who of thy great mercy didst save Noah and his family in the ark from perishing by water; and also didst safely lead the children of Israel, thy people, through the Red Sea, figuring thereby thy holy baptism: and by the baptism of thy well-beloved Son Jesus Christ in the river Jordan, didst sanctify water for this holy sacrament: we beseech thee, for thine infinite mercies, that thou wilt look upon *this child:* wash *him* and sanctify *him* with the Holy Ghost; that *he*, being delivered from thy wrath, may be received into the ark of Christ's Church, and being steadfast in faith, joyful through hope, and rooted in love, may so pass the waves of this troublesome world, that finally *he* may come to the land of everlasting life; there to reign with thee, world without end, through Jesus Christ our Lord. *Amen.*

O merciful God, grant that the old Adam in *this child* may be so buried, that the new man may be raised up in *him*. *Amen.*

Grant that all carnal affections may die in *him*, and that all things belonging to the Spirit may live and grow in *him*. *Amen.*

Grant that *he* may have power and strength to have victory, and to triumph against the devil, the world, and the flesh. *Amen.*

Grant that whosoever is dedicated to thee by our office and ministry may also be endued with heavenly virtues, and everlastingly rewarded through thy mercy, O blessed Lord God, who dost live and govern all things, world without end. *Amen.*

Almighty, ever-living God, whose most dearly-beloved Son Jesus Christ, for the forgiveness of our sins, did shed out of his most precious side both water and blood, and gave commandment to his disciples that they should go teach all nations, and baptize them in the name of the Father, and of the Son, and of the Holy Ghost; regard, we beseech thee, the supplications of thy congregation; sanctify this water for this holy sacrament; and grant that *this child* now to be baptized may receive the fullness of thy grace, and ever remain in the number of thy faithful and elect children, through Jesus Christ our Lord. *Amen.*

Then shall the people stand up; and the minister shall say,

Hear the words of the Gospel written by St. Mark in the tenth chapter, at the thirteenth verse.

They brought young children to Christ, that he should touch them. And his disciples rebuked those that brought them; but when Jesus saw it, he was much displeased, and said unto them, Suffer the little children to come unto me, and forbid them not, for of such is the kingdom of God. Verily I say unto you, Whosoever shall not receive the kingdom of God as a little child, he shall not enter therein. And he took them up in his arms, put his hands upon them, and blessed them.

Then the minister shall take the child into his hands, and say to the friends of the child,

Name this child.

And then, naming it after them, he shall sprinkle or pour water upon it, or, if desired, immerse it in water, saying,

N. I baptize thee in the name of the Father, and of the Son, and of the Holy Ghost. *Amen.*

Then shall be said, all kneeling,

Our Father who art in heaven, hallowed be thy name; thy kingdom come; thy will be done, on earth as it is in heaven: give us this day our daily bread; and forgive us our trespasses, as we forgive them that trespass against us; and lead us not into temptation, but deliver us from evil. *Amen.*

Then sholl the minister conclude with extemporary prayer.

SECTION III.

The Ministration of Baptism to such as are of Riper Years.

Dearly beloved, forasmuch as all men are conceived and born in sin, (and that which is born of the flesh is flesh, and they that are in the flesh cannot please God, but live in sin, committing many actual transgressions:) and that our Saviour Christ saith, None can enter into the kingdom of God, except he be regenerate and born anew of water and of the Holy Ghost: I beseech you to call upon God the Father, through our Lord Jesus Christ, that of his bounteous goodness he will grant to *these persons* that which by nature *they* cannot have; that *they* may be baptized with water and the Holy Ghost, and received into Christ's holy Church, and be made lively *members* of the same.

Then shall the minister say,

Almighty and immortal God, the aid of all that need, the helper of all that flee to thee for succor, the life of them that believe, and the resurrection of the dead: we call upon thee for *these persons;* that *they*, coming to thy holy baptism, may receive remission of *their sins*, by spiritual regeneration. Receive *them*, O Lord, as thou hast promised by thy well-beloved Son, saying, Ask, and ye shall receive; seek, and ye shall find; knock, and it shall be opened unto you: so give now unto us that ask: let us that seek, find: open the gate unto us that knock; that *these persons* may enjoy the everlasting benediction of thy heavenly washing, and may come to the eternal kingdom which thou hast promised by Christ our Lord. *Amen.*

After which he shall say,

Almighty and everlasting God, heavenly Father, we give thee humble thanks, for that thou hast vouchsafed to call us to the knowledge of thy grace, and faith in thee; increase this knowledge and confirm this faith in us evermore. Give thy Holy Spirit to *these persons*, that *they* may be born again, and be made *heirs* of everlasting salvation through our Lord Jesus Christ, who liveth and reigneth with thee and the Holy Spirit, now and for ever. *Amen.*

Then shall the people stand up, and the minister shall say,

Hear the words of the Gospel, written by St. John, in the third chapter, beginning at the first verse.

There was a man of the Pharisees, named Nicodemus, a ruler of the Jews: the same came to Jesus by night, and said unto him, Rabbi, we know that thou art a teacher come from God: for no man can do these miracles that thou doest, except God be with him. Jesus answered and said unto him, Verily, verily, I say unto thee, Except a man be born again, he cannot see the kingdom of God. Nicodemus saith unto him, How can a man be born when he is old? Can he enter the second time into his mother's womb, and be born? Jesus answered, Verily, verily, I say unto thee, Except a man be born of water, and of the Spirit, he cannot enter into the kingdom of God. That which is born of the flesh is flesh; and that which is born of the Spirit is spirit. Marvel not that I said unto thee, Ye must be born again. The wind bloweth where it listeth, and thou hearest the sound thereof, but canst not tell whence it cometh, and whither it goeth: so is every one that is born of the Spirit.

Then the minister shall speak to the persons *to be baptized on this wise:—*

Well beloved, who *are* come hither, desiring to receive holy baptism, *ye* have heard how the congregation hath prayed that our Lord Jesus Christ would vouchsafe to receive you, and bless you, to release you of your sins, to give you the kingdom of heaven, and everlasting life. And our Lord Jesus Christ hath promised, in his holy word, to grant all those things that we have prayed for: which promise he for his part will most surely keep and perform.

Wherefore after this promise made by Christ, *you* must also faithfully, for *your* part, promise, in the presence of this whole congregation, that you will renounce the devil and all his works, and constantly believe God's holy word, and obediently keep his commandments.

Then shall the minister demand of each of the persons to be baptized, severally,

Quest. Dost thou renounce the devil and all his works, the vain pomp and glory of the world, with all covetous desires of the same, and the carnal desires of the flesh, so that thou wilt not follow or be led by them?

Answ. I renounce them all.

Quest. Dost thou believe in God the Father Almighty, Maker of heaven and earth? and in Jesus Christ his only-begotten Son our Lord? and that he was conceived by the Holy Ghost, born of the Virgin Mary? that he suffered under Pontius Pilate, was crucified, dead, and buried: that he rose again the third day; that he ascended into heaven, and sitteth at the right hand of God the Father Almighty, and from thence shall come again, at the end of the world, to judge the quick and the dead?

And dost thou believe in the Holy Ghost, the holy catholic Church,* the communion of saints; the remission of sins; the resurrection of the body, and everlasting life after death?

Answ. All this I steadfastly believe.

* By the holy catholic Church is meant the Church of God in general.

Quest. Wilt thou be baptized in this faith?

Answ. This is my desire.

Quest Wilt thou then obediently keep God's holy will and commandments, and walk in the same all the days of thy life?

Answ. I will endeavor so to do, God being my helper.

Then shall the minister say,

O merciful God, grant that the old Adam in *these persons* may be so buried, that the new man may be raised up in *them*. *Amen.*

Grant that all carnal affections may die in *them*, and that all things belonging to the Spirit may live and grow in *them*. *Amen.*

Grant that *they* may have power and strength to have victory, and triumph against the devil, the world, and the flesh. *Amen.*

Grant that *they* being here dedicated to thee by our office and ministry, may also be endued with heavenly virtues, and everlastingly rewarded, through thy mercy, O blessed Lord God, who dost live and govern all things, world without end. *Amen.*

Almighty, ever-living God, whose most dearly-beloved Son Jesus Christ, for the forgiveness of our sins, did shed out of his most precious side both water and blood; and gave commandment to his disciples that they should go teach all nations, and baptize them in the name of the Father, and of the Son, and of the *Holy Ghost*: *regard*, we beseech thee, the supplications of this congregation; and grant that the *persons* now to be baptized may receive the fullness of thy grace, and ever remain in the number of thy faithful and elect children, through Jesus Christ our Lord. *Amen.*

Then shall the minister take each person to be baptized by the right hand: and placing him conveniently by the font, according to his discretion, shall ask the name; and then shall sprinkle or pour water upon him, (or if he shall desire it, shall immerse him in water,) saying,

N. I baptize thee in the name of the Father, and of the Son, and of the Holy Ghost. *Amen.*

Then shall be said the Lord's Prayer, all kneeling.

Our Father who art in heaven, hallowed be thy name; thy kingdom come; thy will be done on earth, as it is in heaven: give us this day our daily bread; and forgive us our trespasses, as we forgive them that trespass against us: and lead us not into temptation; but deliver us from evil. *Amen.*

[*Then let the minister conclude with extemporary prayer.*]

CHAPTER II.

THE LORD'S SUPPER.

SECTION I.

General Directions.

Quest. ARE there any directions to be given concerning the administration of the Lord's supper?

Answ. 1. Let those who have scruples concerning the receiving of it kneeling, be permitted to receive it either standing or sitting.

2. No person shall be admitted to the Lord's supper among us who is guilty of any practice for which we would exclude a member of our Church.

SECTION II.

The Order for the Administration of the Lord's Supper.

The elder shall say one or more of these sentences:—

Let your light so shine before men, that they may see your good works, and glorify your Father which is in heaven. Matt. v, 16.

Lay not up for yourselves treasures upon earth, where moth and rust doth corrupt, and where thieves break through and steal: but lay up for yourselves treasures in heaven, where neither moth nor rust doth corrupt, and where thieves do not break through nor steal. Matt. vi, 19, 20.

Whatsoever ye would that men should do to you, do ye even so to them: for this is the law and the prophets. Matt. vii, 12.

Not every one that saith unto me, Lord, Lord, shall enter into the kingdom of heaven; but he that doeth the will of my Father which is in heaven. Matt. vii, 21.

Zaccheus stood, and said unto the Lord, Behold, Lord, the half of my goods I give to the poor; and if I have taken anything from any man, by false accusation, I restore him fourfold. Luke xix, 8.

He which soweth sparingly shall reap also sparingly; and he which soweth bountifully shall reap also bountifully. Every man according as he purposeth in his heart, so let him give; not grudgingly, or of necessity: for God loveth a cheerful giver. 2 Cor. ix, 6, 7.

As we have therefore opportunity, let us do good unto all men, especially unto them who are of the household of faith. Gal. vi, 10.

Godliness with contentment is great gain; for we brought nothing into this world, and it is certain we can carry nothing out. 1 Tim. vi, 6, 7.

Charge them that are rich in this world, that they be ready to distribute, willing to communicate, laying up in store for themselves a good foundation against the time to come, that they may lay hold on eternal life. 1 Tim. vi, 17-19.

God is not unrighteous to forget your

work and labor of love, which ye have showed toward his name, in that ye have ministered to the saints, and do minister. Heb. vi, 10.

To do good, and to communicate, forget not: for with such sacrifices God is well pleased. Heb. xiii, 16.

Whoso hath this world's good, and seeth his brother have need, and shutteth up his bowels of compassion from him, how dwelleth the love of God in him? 1 John iii, 17.

He that hath pity upon the poor, lendeth unto the Lord; and that which he hath given will he pay him again. Prov. xix, 17.

Blessed is he that considereth the poor; the Lord will deliver him in time of trouble Psalm xli, 1.

[While these sentences are in reading, some fit person, appointed for that purpose, shall receive the alms for the poor, and other devotions of the people, in a decent basin, to be provided for that purpose; and then bring it to the elder, who shall place it upon the table.]

After which the elder shall say,

Ye that do truly and earnestly repent of your sins, and are in love and charity with your neighbors, and intend to lead a new life, following the commandments of God, and walking from henceforth in his holy ways; draw near with faith, and take this holy sacrament to your comfort: and make your humble confession to Almighty God, meekly kneeling upon your knees.

Then shall this general confession be made by the minister in the name of all those who are minded to receive the holy communion, both he and all the people kneeling humbly upon their knees, and saying,

Almighty God, Father of our Lord Jesus Christ, Maker of all things, Judge of all men: we acknowledge and bewail our manifold sins and wickedness, which we from time to time most grievously have committed, by thought, word, and deed, against thy Divine Majesty, provoking most justly thy wrath and indignation against us. We do earnestly repent, and are heartily sorry for these our misdoings; the remembrance of them is grievous unto us. Have mercy upon us, have mercy upon us, most merciful Father; for thy Son, our Lord Jesus Christ's sake, forgive us all that is past; and grant that we may ever hereafter serve and please thee in newness of life, to the honor and glory of thy name, through Jesus Christ our Lord. *Amen.*

Then shall the elder say,

O Almighty God, our heavenly Father, who of thy great mercy hath promised forgiveness of sins to all them that with hearty repentance and true faith turn unto thee: have mercy upon us; pardon and deliver us from all our sins, confirm and strengthen us in all goodness, and bring us to everlasting life, through Jesus Christ our Lord. *Amen.*

The collect.

Almighty God, unto whom all hearts be open, all desires known, and from whom no secrets are hid; cleanse the thoughts of our hearts by the inspiration of thy Holy Spirit, that we may perfectly love thee, and worthily magnify thy holy name, through Christ our Lord. *Amen.*

Then shall the elder say,

It is very meet, right, and our bounden duty, that we should at all times, and in all places, give thanks unto thee, O Lord, holy Father, almighty, everlasting God.

Therefore with angels and archangels, and with all the company of heaven, we laud and magnify thy glorious name, evermore praising thee, and saying, Holy, holy, holy, Lord God of hosts, heaven and earth are full of thy glory. Glory be to thee, O Lord most high. *Amen.*

Then shall the elder say,

We do not presume to come to this thy table, O merciful Lord, trusting in our own righteousness, but in thy manifold and great mercies. We are not worthy so much as to gather up the crumbs under thy table. But thou art the same Lord, whose property is always to have mercy: Grant us, therefore, gracious Lord, so to eat the flesh of thy dear Son Jesus Christ, and to drink his blood, that our sinful souls and bodies may be made clean by his death, and washed through his most precious blood, and that we may evermore dwell in him, and he in us. *Amen.*

Then the elder shall say the prayer of consecration, as followeth:—

Almighty God, our heavenly Father, who of thy tender mercy didst give thine only Son Jesus Christ to suffer death upon the cross for our redemption; who made there (by his oblation of himself once offered) a full, perfect, and sufficient sacrifice, oblation, and satisfaction, for the sins of the whole world; and did institute, and in his holy gospel command us to continue, a perpetual memory of that his precious death until his coming again: hear us, O merciful Father, we most humbly beseech thee, and grant that we, receiving these thy creatures of bread and wine, according to thy Son our Saviour Jesus Christ's holy institution, in remembrance of his death and passion, may be partakers of his most blessed body and blood; who in the same night that he was betrayed, took bread; (1) and when he had given thanks, he broke it (2) and gave it to his disciples, saying, Take, eat; this (3) is my body which is given for you; do this in remembrance of me.

(1) *Here the elder is to take the plate of bread into his hand.*

(2) *And here to break the bread.*

(3) *And here to lay his hands upon all the bread.*

Likewise after supper he took (4) the cup; and when he had given thanks, he gave it to them, saying, Drink ye all of this: for this (5) is my blood of the New Testament, which is shed for you and for many, for the remission of sins; do this, as oft as ye shall drink it, in remembrance of me. *Amen.*

(4) *Here he is to take the cup in his hand.*

(5) *And here to lay his hand upon all the vessels which contain the wine.*

Then shall the minister first receive the communion in both kinds himself, and then proceed to deliver the same to the other ministers in like manner, (if any be present,) and after that to the people also, in order, into their hands. And when he delivereth the bread, he shall say,

The body of our Lord Jesus Christ, which was given for *thee*, preserve *thy soul* and *body* unto everlasting life. Take and eat this in remembrance that Christ died for *thee*, and feed on him in *thy heart* by faith with thanksgiving.

And the minister that delivereth the cup shall say,

The blood of our Lord Jesus Christ, which was shed for *thee*, preserve *thy soul* and *body* unto everlasting life. Drink this in remembrance that Christ's blood was shed for *thee*, and be thankful.

[If the consecrated bread or wine be all spent before all have communicated, the elder may consecrate more, by repeating the prayer of consecration.]

[When all have communicated, the minister shall return to the Lord's table, and place upon it what remaineth of the consecrated elements, covering the same with a fair linen cloth.]

Then shall the elder say the Lord's Prayer; the people repeating after him every petition.

Our Father who art in heaven, hallowed be thy name: thy kingdom come: thy will be done on earth as it is in heaven: give us this day our daily bread; and forgive us our trespasses, as we forgive them that trespass against us: and lead us not into temptation, but deliver us from evil, for thine is the kingdom, and the power, and the glory, for ever and ever. *Amen.*

After which shall be said as followeth:—

O Lord and heavenly Father, we thy humble servants desire thy fatherly goodness mercifully to accept this our sacrifice of praise and thanksgiving; most humbly beseeching thee to grant that, by the merits and death of thy Son Jesus Christ, and through faith in his blood, we and thy whole Church may obtain remission of our sins, and all other benefits of his passion. And here we offer and present unto thee, O Lord, ourselves, our souls and bodies, to be a reasonable, holy, and lively sacrifice unto thee; humbly beseeching thee that all we who are partakers of this holy communion, may be filled with thy grace and heavenly benediction. And although we be unworthy, through our manifold sins, to offer unto thee any sacrifice, yet we beseech thee to accept this our bounden duty and service; not weighing our merits, but pardoning our offenses, through Jesus Christ our Lord: by whom, and with whom, in the unity of the Holy Ghost, all honor and glory be unto thee, O Father Almighty, world without end. *Amen*

Then shall be said,

Glory be to God on high, and on earth peace, good-will toward men. We praise thee, we bless thee, we worship thee, we glorify thee, we give thanks to thee for thy great glory, O Lord God, heavenly King, God the Father Almighty.

O Lord, the only-begotten Son Jesus Christ; O Lord God, Lamb of God, Son of the Father, that takest away the sins of the world, have mercy upon us. Thou that takest away the sins of the world, have mercy upon us. Thou that takest away the sins of the world, receive our prayer. Thou that sittest at the right hand of God the Father, have mercy upon us.

For thou only art holy; thou only art the Lord; thou only, O Christ, with the Holy Ghost, art most high in the glory of God the Father. *Amen.*

Then the elder, if he see it expedient, may put up an extempore prayer; and afterward shall let the people depart with this blessing:—

May the peace of God, which passeth all understanding, keep your hearts and minds in the knowledge and love of God, and of his Son Jesus Christ our Lord: and the blessing of God Almighty, the Father, the Son, and the Holy Ghost, be among you, and remain with you always. *Amen.*

N. B. If the elder be straitened for time, he may omit any part of the service except the prayer of consecration.

CHAPTER III.

FORMS OF ORDINATION.

SECTION I.

The Form of ordaining a Bishop.

The Collect.

Almighty God, who by thy Son Jesus Christ didst give to thy holy apostles many excellent gifts, and didst charge them to feed thy flock; give grace, we beseech thee, to all the ministers and pastors of thy Church, that they may diligently preach thy word and duly administer the godly discipline thereof; and grant to the people that they may obediently follow the same; that all may receive the crown of everlasting glory, through Jesus Christ our Lord. *Amen.*

Then shall be read by one of the elders

The Epistle. Acts xx, 17-35.

From Miletus Paul sent to Ephesus, and called the elders of the Church. And when they were come to him, he said unto them, Ye know from the first day that I came into Asia, after what manner I have been with you at all seasons, serving the Lord with all humility of mind, and with many tears and temptations which befell me by the lying in wait of the Jews; and how I kept back nothing that was profitable unto you, but have showed you, and have taught you publicly and from house to house, testifying both to the Jews and also to the Greeks, repentance toward God, and faith toward our Lord Jesus Christ. And now behold I go bound in the spirit unto Jerusalem, not knowing the things that shall befall me there; save that the Holy Ghost witnesseth in every city, saying that bonds and afflictions abide me. But none of these things move me, neither count I my life dear unto myself, so that I might finish my course with joy, and the ministry which I have received of the Lord Jesus to testify the gospel of the grace of God. And now, behold, I know that ye all, among whom I have gone preaching the kingdom of God, shall see my face no more. Wherefore I take you to record this day, that I am pure from the blood of all men. For I have not shunned to declare unto you all the counsel of God. Take heed, therefore, unto yourselves, and to all the flock, over the which the Holy Ghost hath made you overseers, to feed the Church of God which he hath purchased with his own blood. For I know this, that after my departing shall grievous wolves enter in among you, not sparing the flock. Also of your own selves shall men arise, speaking perverse things, to draw away disciples after them. Therefore watch, and remember that by the space of three years, I ceased not to warn every one night and day with tears. And now, brethren, I commend you to God, and to the word of his grace, which is able to build you up, and to give you an inheritance among all them which are sanctified. I have coveted no man's silver, or gold, or apparel: yea, ye yourselves know that these hands have ministered unto my necessities, and to them that were with me. I have showed you all things, how that so laboring ye ought to support the weak; and to remember the words of the Lord Jesus, how he said, It is more blessed to give than to receive.

Then another shall read

The Gospel. St. John xxi, 15–17.

Jesus saith to Simon Peter, Simon, son of Jonas, lovest thou me more than these? He saith unto him, Yea, Lord; thou knowest that I love thee. He saith unto him, Feed my lambs. He saith to him again the second time, Simon, son of Jonas, lovest thou me? He saith unto him, Yea, Lord; thou knowest that I love thee. He saith unto him, Feed my sheep. He saith unto him the third time, Simon, son of Jonas, lovest thou me? Peter was grieved because he said unto him the third time, Lovest thou me? And he said unto him, Lord, thou knowest all things; thou knowest that I love thee. Jesus saith unto him, Feed my sheep.

Or this: St. Matt. xxviii, 18–20.

Jesus came and spake unto them, saying, All power is given unto me in heaven and in earth. Go ye therefore and teach all nations, baptizing them in the name of the Father, and of the Son, and of the Holy Ghost; teaching them to observe all things whatsoever I have commanded you: and lo, I am with you alway, even unto the end of the world.

After the Gospel and the sermon are ended, the elected person shall be presented by the two elders unto the bishop, saying,

We present unto you this holy man to be ordained a bishop.

Then the bishop shall move the congregation present to pray, saying thus to them:—

Brethren, it is written in the Gospel of St. Luke, that our Saviour Christ continued the whole night in prayer before he did choose and send forth his twelve apostles. It is written also in the Acts of the Apostles, that the disciples who were at Antioch did fast and pray before they laid hands on Paul and Barnabas, and sent them forth. Let us, therefore, following the example of our

Saviour Christ, and his apostles, first fall to prayer before we admit, and send forth this person presented to us, to the work whereunto we trust the Holy Ghost hath called him.

Then shall be said this prayer following:—

Almighty God, Giver of all good things, who by thy Holy Spirit hast appointed divers orders of ministers in thy Church: mercifully behold this thy servant now called to the work and ministry of a bishop, and replenish him so with the truth of thy doctrine, and adorn him with innocency of life, that both by word and deed he may faithfully serve thee in this office, to the glory of thy name, and the edifying and well governing of thy Church, through the merits of our Saviour Jesus Christ, who liveth and reigneth with thee, and the Holy Ghost, world without end. *Amen.*

Then the bishop shall say to him that is to be ordained:—

Brother, forasmuch as the Holy Scripture commands that we should not be hasty in laying on hands, and admitting any person to government in the Church of Christ, which he hath purchased with no less price than the effusion of his own blood; before I admit you to this administration, I will examine you on certain articles, to the end that the congregation present may have a trial, and bear witness how you are minded to behave yourself in the Church of God.

Are you persuaded that you are truly called to this ministration, according to the will of our Lord Jesus Christ?

Answ. I am so persuaded.

The bishop. Are you persuaded that the Holy Scriptures contain sufficiently all doctrine required of necessity for eternal salvation, through faith in Jesus Christ? And are you determined, out of the same Holy Scriptures, to instruct the people committed to your charge, and to teach or maintain nothing as required of necessity to eternal salvation but that which you shall be persuaded may be concluded and proved by the same?

Answ. I am so persuaded and determined, by God's grace.

The bishop. Will you then faithfully exercise yourself in the same Holy Scriptures, and call upon God by prayer for the true understanding of the same, so as you may be able by them to teach and exhort with wholesome doctrine, and to withstand and convince the gainsayers?

Answ. I will so do, by the help of God.

The bishop. Are you ready with faithful diligence to banish and drive away all erroneous and strange doctrines contrary to God's word, and both privately and openly to call upon and encourage others to the same?

Answ. I am ready, the Lord being my helper.

The bishop Will you deny all ungodliness and worldly lust, and live soberly, righteously, and godly, in this present world, that you may show yourself in all things an ex ample of good works unto others, that the adversary may be ashamed, having nothing to say against you?

Answ. I will so do, the Lord being my helper.

The bishop. Will you maintain and set forward, as much as shall lie in you, quietness, love, and peace, among all men: and such as shall be unquiet, disobedient, and criminal, within your district, correct and punish according to such authority as you have by God's word, and as shall be committed unto you?

Answ. I will so do, by the help of God.

The bishop. Will you be faithful in ordaining, sending, or laying hands upon, others?

Answ. I will so be, by the help of God.

The bishop. Will you show yourself gentle, and be merciful for Christ's sake, to poor and needy people, and to all strangers destitute of help?

Answ. I will so show myself, by God's help.

Then the bishop shall say,

Almighty God, our heavenly Father, who hath given you a good will to do all these things, grant also unto you strength and power to perform the same; that he accomplishing in you the good work which he hath begun, you may be found perfect and irreprehensible at the last day, through Jesus Christ our Lord. *Amen.*

Then shall Veni, Creator Spiritus, be said.

Come, Holy Ghost, our souls inspire,
And lighten with celestial fire.
Thou the anointing Spirit art,
Who dost thy sevenfold gifts impart.
Thy blessed unction from above
Is comfort, life, and fire of love.
Enable with perpetual light
The dullness of our blinded sight;
Anoint and cheer our soiled face
With the abundance of thy grace;
Keep far our foes, give peace at home,
Where thou art Guide, no ill can come.
Teach us to know the Father, Son,
And thee of both to be but one;
That through the ages all along,
This may be our endless song:
Praise to thy eternal merit,
Father, Son, and Holy Spirit.

That ended, the bishop shall say,

Lord, hear our prayer.
Answ. And let our cry come unto thee

Bishop. Let us pray.

Almighty God and most merciful Father, who of thine infinite goodness hast given thine only and dearly-beloved Son Jesus

Christ to be our Redeemer, and the author of everlasting life; who after that he had made perfect our redemption by his death, and was ascended into heaven, poured down his gifts abundantly upon men, making some apostles, some prophets, some evangelists, some pastors, and doctors, to the edifying and making perfect his Church: grant, we beseech thee, to this thy servant, such grace that he may evermore be ready to spread abroad thy gospel, the glad tidings of reconciliation with thee, and use the authority given him, not to destruction, but to salvation; not to hurt, but to help; so that as a wise and faithful servant, giving to the family their portion in due season, he may at last be received into everlasting joy, through Jesus Christ our Lord, who, with thee and the Holy Ghost, liveth and reigneth, one God, world without end. *Amen.*

Then the bishop and elders present shall lay their hands upon the head of the elected person, kneeling before them upon his knees, the bishop saying,

Receive the Holy Ghost for the office and work of a bishop in the Church of God now committed unto thee by the imposition of our hands, in the name of the Father, and of the Son, and of the Holy Ghost.—*Amen.* And remember that thou stir up the grace of God which is given thee by this imposition of our hands; for God hath not given us the spirit of fear, but of power, and love, and soberness.

Then the bishop shall deliver him the Bible, saying,

Give heed unto reading, exhortation, and doctrine. Think upon the things contained in this book. Be diligent in them, that the increase coming thereby may be manifest unto all men. Take heed unto thyself, and to thy doctrine; for by so doing thou shalt both save thyself and them that hear thee. Be to the flock of Christ a shepherd, not a wolf: feed them, devour them not. Hold up the weak, heal the sick, bind up the broken, bring again the outcast, seek the lost, be so merciful that you may not be too remiss; so minister discipline that you forget not mercy; that when the chief Shepherd shall appear, you may receive the never-fading crown of glory, through Jesus Christ our Lord. *Amen.*

[Then the bishop shall administer the Lord's supper, with whom the newly-ordained bishop and other persons present shall communicate.]

Immediately before the benediction shall be said the following prayers:—

Most merciful Father, we beseech thee to send down upon this thy servant thy heavenly blessing, and so endue him with thy Holy Spirit, that he, preaching thy word, may not only be earnest to reprove, beseech, and rebuke with all patience and doctrine, but also may be to such as believe a wholesome example in word, in conversation, in love, in faith, in chastity, and in purity: that faithfully fulfilling his course, at the latter day he may receive the crown of righteousness laid up by the Lord, the righteous Judge, who liveth and reigneth, one God with the Father and the Holy Ghost, world without end. *Amen.*

Prevent us, O Lord, in all our doings with thy most gracious favor, and further us with thy continual help, that in all our works begun, continued, and ended in thee, we may glorify thy holy name; and finally, by thy mercy, obtain everlasting life through Jesus Christ our Lord. *Amen.*

The peace of God which passeth all understanding, keep your hearts and minds in the knowledge and love of God, and of his Son Jesus Christ our Lord; and the blessing of God Almighty, the Father, the Son, and the Holy Ghost, be among you, and remain with you always. *Amen.*

SECTION II.

The Form and Manner of ordaining Elders.

[When the day appointed by the bishop is come, there shall be a sermon or exhortation, declaring the duty and office of such as come to be admitted elders; how necessary that order is in the Church of Christ, and also how the people ought to esteem them in their office.]

After which, one of the elders shall present unto the bishop all them that are to be ordained, and say,

I present unto you these persons present to be ordained elders.

Then their names being read aloud, the bishop shall say unto the people,

Brethren, these are they whom we purpose, God willing, this day to ordain elders. For after due examination, we find not to the contrary, but that they are lawfully called to this function and ministry, and that they are persons meet for the same. But if there be any of you who knoweth any impediment or crime in any of them, for the which he ought not to be received into this holy ministry, let him come forth in the name of God, and show what the crime or impediment is.

[If any crime or impediment be objected, the bishop shall surcease from ordaining that person until such time as the party accused shall be found clear of the crime.]

Then shall be said the collect, epistle, and gospel, as followeth.

The Collect.

Almighty God, Giver of all good things, who by thy Holy Spirit hast appointed divers orders of ministers in thy Church; mercifully behold these thy servants now called to the office of elders, and replenish them so with the truth of thy doctrine, and adorn them with innocency of life, that both by word and good example they may faithfully serve thee in this office, to the glory of thy name, and the edification of thy Church, through the merits of our Saviour

Jesus Christ, who liveth and reigneth with thee and the Holy Ghost, world without end. *Amen.*

The Epistle. Eph. iv, 7-13.

Unto every one of us is given grace according to the measure of the gift of Christ. Wherefore he saith, when he ascended up on high, he led captivity captive, and gave gifts unto men. (Now that he ascended, what is it but that he also descended first into the lower parts of the earth? He that descended is the same also that ascended up far above all heavens, that he might fill all things.) And he gave some, apostles; and some, prophets; and some, evangelists; and some pastors and teachers; for the perfecting of the saints, for the work of the ministry, for the edifying of the body of Christ, till we all come in the unity of the faith, and of the knowledge of the Son of God, unto a perfect man, unto the measure of the stature of the fullness of Christ.

After this shall be read for the Gospel, part of the tenth chapter of St. John.

St. John x, 1-16.

Verily, verily, I say unto you, He that entereth not by the door into the sheepfold, but climbeth up some other way, the same is a thief and a robber. But he that entereth in by the door is the shepherd of the sheep. To him the porter openeth, and the sheep hear his voice, and he calleth his own sheep by name, and leadeth them out. And when he putteth forth his own sheep, he goeth before them, and the sheep follow him, for they know his voice. And a stranger will they not follow, but will flee from him, for they know not the voice of strangers. This parable spake Jesus unto them, but they understood not what things they were which he spake unto them. Then said Jesus unto them again, Verily, verily, I say unto you, I am the door of the sheep. All that ever came before me are thieves and robbers, but the sheep did not hear them. I am the door; by me if any man enter in, he shall be saved, and shall go in and out and find pasture. The thief cometh not but for to steal, and to kill, and to destroy; I am come that they might have life, and that they might have it more abundantly. I am the good shepherd: the good shepherd giveth his life for the sheep. But he that is a hireling, and not the shepherd, whose own the sheep are not, seeth the wolf coming, and leaveth the sheep, and fleeth, and the wolf catcheth them, and scattereth the sheep. The hireling fleeth because he is a hireling, and careth not for the sheep. I am the good shepherd, and know my sheep, and am known of mine. As the Father knoweth me, even so know I the Father: and I lay down my life for the sheep. And other sheep I have which are not of this fold: them also I must bring, and they shall hear my voice, and there shall be one fold and one shepherd.

And that done, the bishop shall say unto them as hereafter followeth :—

You have heard, brethren, as well in your private examination as in the exhortation which was now made to you, and in the holy lessons taken out of the Gospel, and the writings of the apostles, of what dignity and of how great importance this office is whereunto ye are called. And now again we exhort you in the name of our Lord Jesus Christ, that you have in remembrance, into how high a dignity and to how weighty an office ye are called: that is to say, to be messengers, watchmen, and stewards, of the Lord, to teach and to premonish, to feed, and provide for the Lord's family, to seek for Christ's sheep that are dispersed abroad, and for his children who are in the midst of this evil world, that they may be saved through Christ for ever.

Have always therefore printed in your remembrance how great a treasure is committed to your charge. For they are the sheep of Christ, which he bought with his death, and for whom he shed his blood. The Church and congregation whom you must serve, is his spouse and his body. And if it shall happen, the same Church, or any member thereof, do take any hurt or hinderance by reason of your negligence, ye know the greatness of the fault, and also the horrible punishment that will ensue. Wherefore consider with yourselves the end of the ministry toward the children of

God, toward the spouse and body of Christ; and see that you never cease your labor, your care and diligence, until you have done all that lieth in you, according to your bounden duty, to bring all such as are or shall be committed to your charge, unto that agreement in the faith and knowledge of God, and to that ripeness and perfectness of age in Christ, that there be no place left among you, either for error in religion, or for viciousness in life.

Forasmuch then as your office is both of so great excellency, and of so great difficulty, ye see with how great care and study ye ought to apply yourselves, as well that ye may show yourselves dutiful and thankful unto that Lord who hath placed you in so high a dignity; as also to beware that neither you yourselves offend, nor be occasion that others offend. Howbeit ye cannot have a mind and will thereto of yourselves; for that will and ability is given of God alone; therefore ye ought, and have need to pray earnestly for his Holy Spirit. And seeing that ye cannot by any other means compass the doing of so weighty a work, pertaining to the salvation of man, but with doctrine and exhortation taken out of the Holy Scriptures, and with a life agreeable to the same; consider how studious ye ought to be in reading and learning the Scriptures, and in framing the manners, both of yourselves and of them that specially pertain unto you, according to the rule of the same Scriptures; and for this selfsame cause, how ye ought to forsake and set aside (as much as you may) all worldly cares and studies.

We have good hope that you have all weighed and pondered these things with yourselves long before this time: and that you have clearly determined, by God's grace, to give yourselves wholly to this office, whereunto it hath pleased God to call you: so that, as much as lieth in you, you will apply yourselves wholly to this one thing, and draw all your cares and studies this way, and that you will continually pray to God the Father, by the mediation of our only Saviour Jesus Christ, for the heavenly assistance of the Holy Ghost; that by daily reading and weighing of the Scriptures, ye may wax riper and stronger in your ministry; and that ye may so endeavor yourselves from time to time to sanctify the lives of you and yours, and to fashion them after the rule and doctrine of Christ, that ye may be wholesome and godly examples and patterns for the people to follow.

And now that this present congregation of Christ, here assembled, may also understand your minds and wills in these things, and that this your promise may the more move you to do your duties: ye shall answer plainly to these things which we, in the name of God and his Church, shall demand of you touching the same.

Do you think in your heart that you are truly called, according to the will of our Lord Jesus Christ, to the order of elders?

Answ. I think so.

The bishop. Are you persuaded that the Holy Scriptures contain sufficiently all doctrine required of necessity for eternal salvation through faith in Jesus Christ? And are you determined out of the said Scriptures to instruct the people committed to your charge, and to teach nothing as required of necessity to eternal salvation, but that which you shall be persuaded may be concluded and proved by the Scripture?

Answ. I am so persuaded, and have so determined, by God's grace.

The bishop. Will you then give your faithful diligence always so to minister the doctrine and sacraments, and discipline of Christ, as the Lord hath commanded?

Answ. I will so do, by the help of the Lord.

The bishop. Will you be ready with all faithful diligence to banish and drive away all erroneous and strange doctrines contrary to God's word; and to use both public and private monitions and exhortations, as well to the sick as to the whole within your charge, as need shall require and occasion shall be given?

Answ. I will, the Lord being my helper.

The bishop. Will you be diligent in prayers, and in reading of the Holy Scriptures, and in such studies as help to the knowledge of the same, laying aside the study of the world and the flesh?

Answ. I will endeavor so to do, the Lord being my helper.

The bishop. Will you be diligent to frame

and fashion yourselves, and your families, according to the doctrine of Christ: and to make both yourselves and them, as much as in you lieth, wholesome examples and patterns to the flock of Christ?

Answ. I shall apply myself thereto, the Lord being my helper.

The bishop. Will you maintain and set forward, as much as lieth in you, quietness, peace, and love, among all Christian people, and especially among them that are or shall be committed to your charge?

Answ. I will so do, the Lord being my helper.

The bishop. Will you reverently obey your chief ministers, unto whom is committed the charge and government over you; following with a glad mind and will their godly admonitions, submitting yourselves to their godly judgments?

Answ. I will so do, the Lord being my helper.

Then shall the bishop, standing up, say,

Almighty God, who hath given you this will to do all these things, grant also unto you strength and power to perform the same; that he may accomplish his work which he hath begun in you, through Jesus Christ our Lord. *Amen.*

[After this the congregation shall be desired secretly in their prayers to make their humble supplications to God for all these things: for the which prayers there shall be silence kept for a space.]

After which shall be said by the bishop, (the persons to be ordained elders all kneeling,) Veni, Creator Spiritus, *the bishop beginning, and the elders and others that are present answering by verse, as followeth :—*

Come, Holy Ghost, our souls inspire,
And lighten with celestial fire.
Thou the anointing Spirit art,
Who dost thy sevenfold gifts impart.
Thy blessed unction from above
Is comfort, life, and fire of love.
Enable with perpetual light
The dullness of our blinded sight,
Anoint and cheer our soiled face
With the abundance of thy grace:
Keep far our foes, give peace at home,
Where thou art guide no ill can come:
Teach us to know the Father, Son,
And thee of both to be but one:
That through the ages all along,
This may be our endless song:
Praise to thy eternal merit,
Father, Son, and Holy Spirit.

That done, the bishop shall pray in this wise, and say,

Let us pray.

Almighty God and heavenly Father, who of thine infinite love and goodness toward us, hast given to us thy only and most dearly beloved Son Jesus Christ to be our Redeemer, and the author of everlasting life; who, after he had made perfect our redemption by his death, and was ascended into heaven, sent abroad into the world his apostles, prophets, evangelists, doctors, and pastors, by whose labor and ministry he gathered together a great flock in all parts of the world, to set forth the eternal praise of thy holy name: for these so great benefits of thy eternal goodness, and for that thou hast vouchsafed to call these thy servants here present to the same office and ministry appointed for the salvation of mankind, we render unto thee most hearty thanks: we praise and worship thee; and we humbly beseech thee by the same, thy blessed Son, to grant unto all who either here or elsewhere call upon thy name, that we may continue to show ourselves thankful unto thee for these, and all other thy benefits, and that we may daily increase and go forward in the knowledge and faith of thee and thy Son, by the Holy Spirit. So that as well by these thy ministers, as by them over whom they shall be appointed thy ministers, thy holy name may be for ever glorified, and thy blessed kingdom enlarged, through the same, thy Son Jesus Christ our Lord: who liveth and reigneth with thee in the unity of the same Holy Spirit, world without end. *Amen.*

When this prayer is done, the bishop, with the elders present, shall lay their hands severally upon the head of every one that receiveth the order of elders; the receivers humbly kneeling upon their knees, and the bishop saying,

The Lord pour upon thee the Holy Ghost for the office and work of an elder in the

Church of God, now committed unto thee by the imposition of our hands. And be thou a faithful dispenser of the word of God, and of his holy sacraments; in the name of the Father, and of the Son, and of the Holy Ghost. *Amen.*

Then the bishop shall deliver to every one of them, kneeling, the Bible into his hands, saying,

Take thou authority to preach the word of God, and to administer the holy sacraments in the congregation.

Then the bishop shall say,

Most merciful Father, we beseech thee to send upon these thy servants thy heavenly blessings, that they may be clothed with righteousness, and that thy word spoken by their mouths may have such success, that it may never be spoken in vain. Grant also that we may have grace to hear and receive what they shall deliver out of thy most holy word, or agreeably to the same, as the means of our salvation; and that in all our words and deeds we may seek thy glory, and the increase of thy kingdom, through Jesus Christ our Lord. *Amen.*

Prevent us, O Lord, in all our doings, with thy most gracious favor, and further us with thy continual help, that in all our works begun, continued, and ended in thee, we may glorify thy holy name, and finally, by thy mercy, obtain everlasting life, through Jesus Christ our Lord. *Amen.*

The peace of God which passeth all understanding, keep your hearts and minds in the knowledge and love of God, and of his Son Jesus Christ our Lord; and the blessing of God Almighty, the Father, the Son, and the Holy Ghost, be among you, and remain with you always. *Amen.*

*** [If on the same day the order of deacons be given to some, and that of elders to others, the deacons shall be first presented, and then the elders. The collects shall both be used: first that for deacons, then that for elders. The epistle shall be Ephes. iv, 7 to 13, as before in this office. Immediately after which, they that are to be ordained deacons shall be examined and ordained as is above prescribed Then one of them having read the Gospel, which shall be St. John x, 1, as before in this office; they that are to be ordained elders shall likewise be examined and ordained, as in this office before appointed.]

SECTION III.

The Form and Manner of making of Deacons.

[When the day appointed by the bishop is come, there shall be a sermon or exhortation, declaring the duty and office of such as come to be admitted deacons.]

After which, one of the elders shall present unto the bishop the persons to be ordained deacons, and their names being read aloud, the bishop shall say unto the people:—

Brethren, if there be any of you who knoweth any impediment or crime in any of these persons presented to be ordained deacons, for the which he ought not to be admitted to that office, let him come forth in the name of God, and show what the crime or impediment is.

[If any crime or impediment be objected, the bishop shall surcease from ordaining that person until such time as the party accused shall be found clear of that crime.]

Then shall be read the following collect and epistle :—

The Collect.

Almighty God, who by thy divine Providence hast appointed divers orders of ministers in thy Church, and didst inspire thy apostles to choose into the order of deacons thy first martyr, St. Stephen, with others: mercifully behold these thy servants, now called to the like office and administration; replenish them so with the truth of thy doctrine, and adorn them with innocency of life, that both by word and good example they may faithfully serve thee in this office to the glory of thy name, and the edification of thy Church, through the merits of our Saviour Jesus Christ, who liveth and reigneth with thee and the Holy Ghost now and for ever. *Amen.*

The Epistle. 1 Tim. iii, 8–13.

Likewise must the deacons be grave, not double tongued, not given to much wine, not greedy of filthy lucre; holding the mystery of the faith in a pure conscience. And let these also first be proved; then let them use the office of a deacon, being found blameless. Even so must their wives be grave, not slanderers, sober, faithful in all things. Let the deacons be the husbands of one wife, ruling their children and their own houses well. For they that have used the office of a deacon well, purchase to themselves a good degree, and great boldness in the faith which is in Christ Jesus.

Then shall the bishop examine every one of those who are to be ordained, in the presence of the people, after this manner following:—

Do you trust that you are inwardly moved by the Holy Ghost to take upon you the office of the ministry in the Church of Christ, to serve God for the promoting of his glory and the edifying of his people?

Answ. I trust so.

The bishop. Do you unfeignedly believe all the canonical Scriptures of the Old and New Testament?

Answ. I do believe them.

The bishop. Will you diligently read or expound the same unto the people whom you shall be appointed to serve?

Answ. I will.

The bishop. It appertaineth to the office of a deacon to assist the elder in divine service. And especially when he ministereth the holy communion, to help him in the distribution thereof, and to read and expound the Holy Scriptures; to instruct the youth, and in the absence of the elder to baptize. And furthermore, it is his office to search for the sick, poor, and impotent, that they may be visited and relieved. Will you do this gladly and willingly?

Answ. I will do so by the help of God.

The bishop. Will you apply all your diligence to frame and fashion your own lives (and the lives of your families) according to the doctrine of Christ; and to make (both) yourselves, (and them,) as much as in you lieth, wholesome examples of the flock of Christ?

Answ. I will do so, the Lord being my helper.

The bishop. Will you reverently obey them to whom the charge and government over you is committed, following with a glad mind and will their godly admonitions?

Answ. I will endeavor so to do, the Lord being my helper.

Then the bishop, laying his hands severally upon the head of every one of them, shall say,

Take thou authority to execute the office of a deacon in the Church of God; in the name of the Father, and of the Son, and the Holy Ghost. *Amen.*

Then shall the bishop deliver to every one of them the Holy Bible, saying,

Take thou authority to read the Holy Scriptures in the Church of God, and to preach the same.

Then one of them appointed by the bishop shall read the Gospel.

Luke xii, 35–38.

Let your loins be girded about, and your lights burning, and ye yourselves like unto men that wait for their Lord, when he will return from the wedding, that when he cometh and knocketh, they may open unto him immediately. Blessed are those servants whom the Lord when he cometh shall find watching. Verily I say unto you, that he shall gird himself, and make them to sit down to meat, and will come forth and serve them. And if he shall come in the second watch, or come in the third watch, and find them so, blessed are those servants.

[Then shall the bishop proceed in the communion, and all that are ordained shall receive the holy communion.]

The communion ended, immediately before the benediction shall be said these collects following:—

Almighty God, Giver of all good things, who of thy great goodness hast vouchsafed to accept and take these thy servants into the office of deacons in thy Church: make them, we beseech thee, O Lord, to be modest, humble, and constant in their ministration, and to have a ready will to observe all spiritual discipline; that they having always the testimony of a good conscience, and continuing ever stable and strong in thy Son Christ, may so well behave themselves in this inferior office, that they may be found worthy to be called into the higher ministries in thy Church, through the same, thy Son our Saviour Jesus Christ; to whom be glory and honor, world without end. *Amen.*

Prevent us, O Lord, in all our doings, with thy most gracious favor, and further us with thy continual help; that in all our works, begun, continued, and ended in thee, we may glorify thy holy name, and finally, by thy mercy, obtain everlasting life, through Jesus Christ our Lord. *Amen.*

The peace of God, which passeth all understanding, keep your hearts and minds in the knowledge and love of God, and of his Son Jesus Christ our Lord. And the blessing of God Almighty, the Father, the Son, and the Holy Ghost, be among you, and remain with you always. *Amen.*

CHAPTER IV.

THE FORM OF SOLEMNIZATION OF MATRIMONY.

First, the banns of all that are to be married together must be published in the congregation three several Sundays in the time of divine service, (unless they be otherwise qualified according to law,) the minister saying after the accustomed manner,

I PUBLISH the banns of marriage between *M.* of ——, and *N.* of ——. If any of you know cause or just impediment why these two persons should not be joined together in holy matrimony, *ye* are to declare it. This is the first [*second or third*] time of asking.

At the day and time appointed for solemnization of matrimony, the persons to be married standing together, the man on the right hand, and the woman on the left, the minister shall say,

Dearly beloved, we are gathered together here in the sight of God, and in the presence of these witnesses, to join together this man and this woman in holy matrimony: which is an honorable estate, instituted of God in the time of man's innocency, signifying unto us the mystical union that is between Christ and his Church; which holy estate Christ adorned and beautified with his presence, and first miracle that he wrought in Cana of Galilee, and is commended of St. Paul to be honorable among all men; and therefore is not by any to be enterprised, or taken in hand unadvisedly, but reverently, discreetly, advisedly, and in the fear of God.

Into which holy estate these two persons present come now to be joined. Therefore, if any can show any just cause why they may not lawfully be joined together, let him now speak, or else hereafter for ever hold his peace.

And also speaking unto the persons that are to be married, he shall say,

I require and charge you both (as you will answer at the dreadful day of judgment, when the secrets of all hearts shall be disclosed) that if either of you know any impediment why you may not be lawfully joined together in matrimony, you do now confess it: for be ye well assured, that so many as are coupled together otherwise than God's word doth allow, are not joined together by God, neither is their matrimony lawful.

If no impediment be alledged, then shall the minister say unto the man,

M., Wilt thou have this woman to thy wedded wife, to live together after God's ordinance, in the holy estate of matrimony? Wilt thou love her, comfort her, honor, and keep her, in sickness and in health: and, forsaking all other, keep thee only unto her, so long as ye both shall live?

The man shall answer

I will.

Then shall the minister say unto the woman,

N., Wilt thou have this man to thy wedded husband, to live together after God's ordinance, in the holy estate of matrimony? Wilt thou obey him, serve him, love, honor, and keep him, in sickness and in health; and, forsaking all other, keep thee only unto him, so long as ye both shall live?

The woman shall answer,

I will.

Then the minister shall cause the man with his right hand to take the woman by her right hand, and to say after him as followeth:—

I *M.* take thee *N.* to be my wedded wife, to have and to hold, from this day forward, for better, for worse, for richer, for poorer, in sickness and in health, to love and to cherish, till death us do part, according to God's holy ordinance: and thereto I plight thee my faith.

Then shall they loose their hands, and the woman with her right hand taking the man by his right hand, shall likewise say after the minister :—

I *N.* take thee *M.* to be my wedded husband, to have and to hold from this day forward, for better, for worse, for richer, for poorer, in sickness and in health, to love, cherish, and to obey, till death us do part, according to God's holy ordinance: and thereto I give thee my faith.

Then shall the minister say,

Let us pray.

O, eternal God, Creator and Preserver of all mankind, Giver of all spiritual grace, the Author of everlasting life ; send thy blessing upon these thy servants, this man and this woman, whom we bless in thy name ; that as Isaac and Rebecca lived faithfully together, so these persons may surely perform and keep the vow and covenant between them made, and may ever remain in perfect love and peace together, and live according to thy laws, through Jesus Christ our Lord *Amen.*

Then shall the minister join their right hands together, and say,

Those whom God hath joined together let no man put asunder.

Forasmuch as *M.* and *N.* have consented together in holy wedlock, and have witnessed the same before God and this company, and thereto have pledged their faith either to other, and have declared the same by joining of hands; I pronounce that they are man and wife together, in the name of the Father, and of the Son, and of the Holy Ghost. *Amen.*

And the minister shall add this blessing :—

God the Father, God the Son, God the Holy Ghost, bless, preserve, and keep you; the Lord mercifully with his favor look upon you, and so fill you with all spiritual benediction and grace, that ye may so live together in this life, that in the world to come ye may have life everlasting. *Amen.*

Then the minister shall say,

Our Father who art in heaven, hallowed be thy name; thy kingdom come; thy will be done on earth, as it is in heaven: give us this day our daily bread; and forgive us our trespasses, as we forgive them that trespass against us: and lead us not into temptation; but deliver us from evil. *Amen.*

Then shall the minister say,

O God of Abraham, God of Isaac, God of

Jacob, bless this man and this woman, and sow the seed of eternal life in their hearts, that whatsoever in thy holy word they shall profitably learn, they may indeed fulfill the same. Look, O Lord, mercifully on them from heaven, and bless them: and as thou didst send thy blessings upon Abraham and Sarah, to their great comfort, so vouchsafe to send thy blessings upon this man and this woman, that they, obeying thy will, and always being in safety under thy protection, may abide in thy love unto their lives' end, through Jesus Christ our Lord. *Amen.*

O God, who by thy mighty power hast made all things of nothing; who also (after other things set in order) didst appoint that out of man (created after thine own image and similitude) woman should take her beginning; and knitting them together, didst teach that it should never be lawful to put asunder those whom thou, by matrimony, hadst made one: O God, who hast consecrated the state of matrimony to such an excellent mystery, that in it is signified and represented the spiritual marriage and unity between Christ and his Church: look mercifully upon this man and this woman; that this man may love his wife, according to thy word, (as Christ did love his spouse, the Church, who gave himself for it; loving and cherishing it, even as his own flesh,) and also that this woman may be loving and amiable, faithful and obedient to her husband; and in all quietness, sobriety, and peace, be a follower of holy and godly matrons. O Lord, bless them both, and grant them to inherit thy everlasting kingdom, through Jesus Christ our Lord. *Amen.*

Then shall the minister say.

Almighty God, who at the beginning did create our first parents, Adam and Eve, and did sanctify and join them together in marriage, pour upon you the riches of his grace, sanctify and bless you, that ye may please him both in body and soul, and live together in holy love unto your lives' end. *Amen.*

CHAPTER V.

ORDER OF THE BURIAL OF THE DEAD.

The minister, meeting the corpse, and going before it, shall say,

I AM the resurrection and the life: he that believeth in me, though he were dead, yet shall he live: and whosoever liveth and believeth in me, shall never die. John xi, 25, 26.

I know that my Redeemer liveth, and that he shall stand at the latter day upon the earth: and though after my skin worms destroy this body, yet in my flesh shall I see God: whom I shall see for myself, and mine eyes shall behold, and not another. Job xix, 25–27.

We brought nothing into this world, and it is certain we can carry nothing out. The Lord gave, and the Lord hath taken away, blessed be the name of the Lord. 1 Tim. vi, 7; Job i, 21.

At the grave, when the corpse is laid in the earth, the minister shall say,

Man that is born of a woman hath but a short time to live, and is full of misery. He cometh up, and is cut down like a flower: he fleeth as it were a shadow, and never continueth in one stay.

In the midst of life we are in death: of whom may we seek for succor, but of thee, O Lord, who for our sins art justly displeased?

Yet, O Lord God most holy, O Lord most mighty, O holy and most merciful Saviour, deliver us not into the bitter pains of eternal death.

Thou knowest, Lord, the secrets of our hearts: shut not thy merciful ears to our prayers, but spare us, Lord most holy, O God most mighty, O holy and merciful Saviour, thou most worthy Judge eternal, suffer us not at our last hour for any pains of death to fall from thee.

Then shall be said,

I heard a voice from heaven saying unto me, Write; from henceforth blessed are the dead who die in the Lord: even so, saith the Spirit; for they rest from their labors.

Then shall the minister say,

Lord have mercy upon us.
Christ have mercy upon us.
Lord have mercy upon us.

Our Father who art in heaven, hallowed be thy name; thy kingdom come; thy will be done on earth as it is in heaven: give us this day our daily bread, and forgive us our trespasses, as we forgive them that trespass against us: and lead us not into temptation; but deliver us from evil. *Amen.*

The Collect.

O merciful God, the Father of our Lord Jesus Christ, who is the resurrection and the life; in whom whosoever believeth shall live, though he die: and whosoever liveth and believeth in him, shall not die eternally. We meekly beseech thee, O Father, to raise us from the death of sin unto the life of righteousness; that when we shall depart this life we may rest in him; and at the general resurrection on the last day may be found acceptable in thy sight, and receive that blessing which thy well-beloved Son shall then pronounce to all that love and fear thee, saying, Come ye blessed children of my Father, receive the kingdom prepared for you from the beginning of the world. Grant this, we beseech thee, O merciful Father, through Jesus Christ our Mediator and Redeemer. *Amen.*

The grace of our Lord Jesus Christ, and the love of God, and the fellowship of the Holy Ghost, be with us all evermore. *Amen.*

PART III.

Temporal Economy.

CHAPTER I.

OF THE BOUNDARIES OF THE ANNUAL CONFERENCES.

1. The NEW-YORK CONFERENCE shall consist of the territory now included in the New-York, Poughkeepsie, Rhinebeck, Delaware, and Newburg Districts.

2. The NEW-YORK EAST CONFERENCE shall consist of the East New-York, the New-Haven, the Hartford, and the Long Island Districts, including in the city of New-York, all those charges lying east of a line running through the Third Avenue, Bowery, Chatham-street, and Broadway.

3. The PROVIDENCE CONFERENCE shall include that part of the State of Connecticut lying east of the Connecticut River, all the State of Rhode Island, with Millville and Blackstone stations in Massachusetts, and also that part of the State of Massachusetts lying south-east of a line drawn from the north-east corner of the State of Rhode Island to the mouth of the Neponset River, which line shall so run as to leave Walpole station and Quincy Point within the bounds of the New-England Conference.

4. NEW-ENGLAND CONFERENCE shall include all the State of Massachusetts lying east of the Green Mountains, not embraced in the New-Hampshire and Providence Conferences.

5. The MAINE CONFERENCE shall include that part of the State of Maine lying west of the Kennebeck River, from the mouth to the Great Bend below Skowhegan, and of a line running from thence north to the State line, (including Skowhegan and Augusta stations in Maine Conference,) and that part of New-Hampshire lying east of the White Hills, and north of the waters of the Ossipee Lake.

6. The EAST MAINE CONFERENCE shall include that part of the State of Maine not included in the Maine Conference.

7. The NEW-HAMPSHIRE CONFERENCE shall include all the State of New-Hampshire not embraced in the Maine Conference, and that part of the State of Massachusetts north-east of the Merrimack River.

8. The VERMONT CONFERENCE shall include the State of Vermont, except that part lying west of the top of the Green Mountains, embraced in the Troy Conference.

9. The TROY CONFERENCE shall include the Troy, Albany, (embracing Richmondville station,) Saratoga, Poultney, Burlington, Plattsburg, and St. Albans Districts.

10. The BLACK RIVER CONFERENCE shall include, together with Rose Circuit, that part of the State of New-York west of

the Troy Conference, not embraced in the East Genesee Conference, as far south as the Erie Canal, and all the societies on the immediate banks of said canal, except Utica, Canistota, Montezuma, and Port Byron.

11. The ONEIDA CONFERENCE shall include that part of the State of New-York south of the Black River Conference, and east of Cayuga Lake, and north of a line running east from Newfield to Ithaca. From thence, following the Catskill turnpike to Greene, and from thence following the same line of road through Masonville to the New-York Conference, including all the charges through which said line passes. From thence on the west line of the Troy Conference to the Erie Canal, including Fort Plain.

12. The WYOMING CONFERENCE shall include that part of the State of New-York not included in the Oneida, East Genesee, and New-York Conferences, and the Susquehanna and Wyoming Districts in the State of Pennsylvania, including Stoddartsville circuit.

13. The EAST GENESEE CONFERENCE shall contain all that part of the State of New-York, west of Black River, Oneida, and Wyoming Conferences, and east of the Genesee River, excepting Lima station, including the city of Rochester, together with so much of the State of Pennsylvania as is included in the Elmira and Corning Districts.

14. The GENESEE CONFERENCE shall

include all that part of the State of New-York, including Lima station, west of the East Genesee Conference, except so much as is included in the Erie Annual Conference, and also Smithport, Cudersport, and Bradford circuits, in Pennsylvania.

15. The ERIE CONFERENCE shall be bounded on the north by Lake Erie, on the east by a line commencing at the mouth of Cattaraugus Creek, thence up said creek to the village of Lodi, leaving said village in the Genesee Conference, thence to the Alleghany River, at the mouth of Tunanquant Creek, thence up said creek eastward to the ridge dividing between the waters of Clarion and Sinnamahoning Creeks, thence south to the head of Mahoning Creek, thence down said creek, exclusive of the Milton society, to the Alleghany River, thence across said river in a north-westerly direction to the Western Reserve line, including the north part of Butler and New-Castle circuits, and also including Petersburgh, thence west to the Ohio Canal, thence along said canal to Lake Erie, including Akron and Cleveland city.

16. The PITTSBURGH CONFERENCE shall be bounded on the north by the Erie Conference, on the east by a line running along the tops of the Alleghany Mountains to the southern line of the State of Pennsylvania, thence west along the line of the Western Virginia Conference to the Ohio River, thence down said river to the mouth of the Muskingum River, thence up said river, ex-

clusive of the towns of Marietta and Zanesville, to the Tuscarawas River, thence up said river, exclusive of the town of Massillon, to the line of the Erie Conference.

17. The WESTERN VIRGINIA CONFERENCE shall be bounded as follows:—Beginning at the south-west corner of the Pennsylvania line, thence along said line to the north-east corner of Ohio County, Virginia, so as to include Wheeling Creek mission and Triadelphia circuits; thence the most direct way to Short Creek, so as to include the Short Creek and Liberty circuit, thence down said creek to the Ohio River, thence down said river to the mouth of Big Sandy River, thence up said river, so as to include the Charleston district; on the south and east it shall be bounded by the Baltimore Conference to the Pennsylvania State line, thence westward by said line to the place of beginning.

18. The OHIO CONFERENCE shall commence at the south-east corner of the North Ohio Conference, and thence south, following the course of the Muskingum River to its junction with the Ohio River, including the city of Zanesville, and the town of Marietta, thence down the Ohio River to the mouth of Ohio Brush Creek, thence north to the south-east corner of Fayette County, leaving Sinking Spring circuit and Bethesda and Rapid Forge societies in Highland County, west of this line, and Washington circuit east, except Fairfield, which shall be left west of said line, thence north-west to

the western boundary of said county of Fayette, thence in a due-north direction to the southern boundary of the North Ohio Conference, leaving Vienna circuit west of said line, thence east with the southern line of the North Ohio Conference to the place of beginning.

19. The CINCINNATI CONFERENCE shall commence at the mouth of Ohio Brush Creek, and shall be bounded on the south by the Ohio River, and on the west by the Indiana State line, to the southern bounds of the North Ohio Conference, at the south-west corner of Dark County, thence eastwardly along said line, so as to exclude the Sydney and Delaware districts of the North Ohio Conference, to the boundary of the Ohio Conference at its junction with the southern line of the North Ohio Conference, thence in a south-eastwardly direction with said western line of the Ohio Conference to the place of beginning.

20. The KENTUCKY CONFERENCE shall include the State of Kentucky, excepting so much of said State as is included in the Westerr Virginia Conference.

21. The NORTH OHIO CONFERENCE hall embrace all that part of the State of Ohio not included in the Ohio, Cincinnati, Pittsburgh and Erie Conferences.

22. The MICHIGAN CONFERENCE shall include the State of Michigan.

23. The INDIANA CONFERENCE shall be bounded as follows, viz.:—Beginning at the mouth of Silver Creek, on the Ohio River,

thence with said creek to the Jeffersonville Railroad, thence by said railroad to Rockford, thence by the East Fork of White River to Columbus, thence by the Madison and Indianapolis railroad to Franklin, thence by the Plank Road to the Bluffs of White River, thence north by said river to the southern line of the Donation of Indianapolis, thence east by said line to Meridian-street, thence north by said street to its intersection with Market-street, thence west by Market-street to the Donation line, then south by said Donation line to the National Road, thence by the National Road west to the intersection of the Greencastle State road, one-and-a-half miles west of Stilesville, thence with said State Road to the town plat of Greencastle, thence due south to Seminary-street, thence by said street to College-street, including the second charge in Greencastle, together with lot No. 153, thence due south to the southern border of the college grounds, upon a line equally dividing the college campus and building; thence due west to the Walnut Fork of Eel River, thence down said river to its intersection with the National Road, thence with said road to the western line of the State, including all the towns on the National Road west of Indianapolis in Indiana Conference, except the city of Terre Haute; thence by the State line to the mouth of the Wabash River, thence by the State line to the mouth of Silver Creek, the place of beginning.

24. The NORTH-WESTERN INDIANA CONFERENCE shall embrace all of North-Western Indiana, bounded north by the State and Lake of Michigan, east by the Michigan Road, and St. Joseph River, south by Indiana Conference, and west by the State of Illinois; also the city of Terre Haute, with so much of the city of Indianapolis within the Donation as lies north of Market-street, and west of Meridian-street, with all the towns on the Michigan Road except Logansport.

25. The NORTH INDIANA CONFERENCE shall include all of North-Eastern Indiana, bounded north by Michigan, east by Ohio, south by the National Road, and west by the Michigan Road as far north as South Bend, thence down St. Joseph River to the Michigan State Line; also the town of Logansport, all the towns on the National Road east of Indianapolis, and so much of the city of Indianapolis within the Donation as lies north of Market-street, and east of Meridian-street.

26. The SOUTH-EASTERN INDIANA CONFERENCE shall include all of South-Eastern Indiana, bounded north by the National Road, east by Ohio, south by the Ohio River, and west by the Indiana Conference; so much of the city of Indianapolis within the Donation, as lies south of Market-street and east of Meridian-street, and all the towns and societies on the line between Indiana and South-Eastern Indiana Conferences.

27. The ROCK RIVER CONFERENCE shall include all of the State of Illinois lying north of the line of the Illinois Conference, not included in the Wisconsin Conference.

28. The WISCONSIN CONFERENCE shall include the territory embraced in the State of Wisconsin, with the addition of so much of Council Hill and Monroe circuits as lies within the State of Illinois, and all the territory of Minnesota.

29. The IOWA CONFERENCE shall include the State of Iowa, and the territory of Nebraska; except so much as is occupied by the Indian Mission, now in connexion with the Missouri Conference.

30. The ILLINOIS CONFERENCE shall include that part of Illinois not included in South Illinois Conference, south of the following line, namely: Beginning at Warsaw on the Mississippi River, thence to Vermont, thence to the mouth of Spoon River, thence to the Indiana State line, embracing Warsaw, Vermont, Havana circuit, Bloomington station, and Danville circuit.

31. The SOUTHERN ILLINOIS CONFERENCE shall include all the State of Illinois lying south of the following line—beginning on the Mississippi River at Gilead, in Calhoun County, thence east to the north-west corner of Jersey County, thence with the Northern line of said county, thence with the Macoussin Creek east of Carlinville, thence east to Hillsboro, in Montgomery County, to leave Hillsboro, Carrolton, Greenville, Carlinville, and Hillsboro circuits

within the Illinois Conference; thence east through Fayette and Effingham counties, to the north west corner of Jasper County, thence with the north line of Jasper and Crawford counties, to Wabash River and Indiana State line.

32. The MISSOURI CONFERENCE shall include the State of Missouri, except that part lying south of the Osage River, and west of Miller, Pulaski, and Ashley counties, and that part of the Nebraska territory, embracing the Indian Missions in said territory.

33. The ARKANSAS CONFERENCE shall include the States of Arkansas, Texas, and so much of New-Mexico as lies east of the Rocky Mountains, and that part of the Indian territory west of Arkansas, and so much of the State of Missouri as is not included in the Missouri Conference.

34. The BALTIMORE CONFERENCE shall include all that part of Virginia not embraced in the Western Virginia, Pittsburgh, and Philadelphia Conferences, and which is bounded by a line commencing at the mouth of the Rappahannock River, running with said river to the head waters thereof, (including Fredericksburg,) thence by the Blue Ridge to New River, taking in Floyd Circuit, thence by New River, to the boundary of the Western Virginia Conference; and the western shore of Maryland, except a small portion included in the Western Virginia Conference, and that part of Pennsylvania lying east of the Alleghany Moun-

tains and west of the Susquehanna River, including Huntington and Northumberland districts.

35. The PHILADELPHIA CONFERENCE shall include the Eastern Shore of Maryland and Virginia, the State of Delaware, and all that part of Pennsylvania lying between the Susquehanna and Delaware rivers, except so much as is included in Baltimore, Wyoming, and New-Jersey Conferences.

36. The NEW-JERSEY CONFERENCE shall include the whole State of New-Jersey, Staten Island, and so much of the States of New-York and Pennsylvania as is now included in the Newton and Paterson districts.

37. The OREGON CONFERENCE shall embrace the territory of Oregon.

38. The CALIFORNIA CONFERENCE shall embrace the State of California, the Territory of Utah, and so much of the Territory of New-Mexico as lies west of the Rocky Mountains.

39. The LIBERIA CONFERENCE. There shall be an Annual Conference on the Western Coast of Africa, to be denominated the *Liberia Mission Annual Conference*, possessing all the rights, powers, and privileges of other Annual Conferences, except that of sending delegates to the General Conference, and of drawing its annual dividend from the avails of the Book Concern and of the Charter Fund.

GERMAN WORK.

1. The Pittsburgh, the North Ohio, and the Cincinnati Districts, with the exception of Lawrenceburg, are connected with the Cincinnati Conference.

2. The North Indiana District, as it now is, and the Indiana District, with the addition of Lawrenceburg, are connected with the South-Eastern Indiana Conference.

3. The St. Louis, Missouri, and the Quincy Districts, with the exception of Pekin and Peoria Missions, are connected with the Illinois Conference.

4. The Wisconsin and Iowa Districts, with the addition of Pekin and Peoria Missions, are connected with the Rock River Conference.

5. The German Missions in the east, remain in connexion with the New-York Conference.

CHAPTER II.

OF CHURCHES AND CHURCH PROPERTY.

SECTION I.

Of building Churches, and the Order to be observed therein.

Quest. 1. Is anything advisable in regard to building churches?

Answ. 1. Let all our churches be built

plain and decent, and with free seats whereever practicable;* but not more expensive than is absolutely unavoidable—otherwise the necessity of raising money will make rich men necessary to us. But if so, we must be dependent on them, yea, and governed by them. And then farewell to Methodist discipline, if not doctrine too.

2. In order more effectually to prevent our people from contracting debts which they are not able to discharge, it shall be the duty of the Quarterly Conference, of every circuit and station, where it is contemplated to build a house or houses of worship, to secure the ground or lot on which such house or houses are to be built, according to our deed of settlement, which deed must be legally executed; and also said Quarterly Conference shall appoint a judicious committee of at least three members of our Church, who shall form an estimate of the amount necessary to build; and three-fourths of the money, according to such estimate, shall be secured or subscribed before any such building shall be commenced.

In all cases where debts for building houses of worship have been, or may be, incurred contrary to, or in disregard of, the above recommendation, our members and friends are requested to discountenance, by declining pecuniary aid to all agents who shall travel abroad beyond their own circuits or districts for the collection of funds for the discharge of such debts: except in such peculiar cases as may be approved

* See note on page 210.

by an Annual Conference, or such agents as may be appointed by their authority.

3. In future we will admit no charter, deed, or conveyance, for any house of worship to be used by us, unless it be provided in such charter, deed, or conveyance, that the trustees of said house shall at all times permit such ministers and preachers belonging to the Methodist Episcopal Church as shall from time to time be duly authorized by the General Conference of the ministers of our Church, or by the Annual Conferences, to preach and expound God's holy word, and to execute the discipline of the Church, and to administer the sacraments therein, according to the true meaning and purport of our deed of settlement.

SECTION II.

Of the Form of a Deed of Settlement.[o]

Quest. What shall be done for the security of our preaching-houses, and the premises belonging thereto?

Answ. Let the following plan of a deed of settlement be brought into effect in all possible cases, and as far as the laws of the States respectively will admit of it. But each Annual Conference is authorized to make such modification in the deeds as they may find the different usages and customs of law require in the different States and Territories, so as to secure the premises firmly by deed, and permanently to the Methodist

[o] For the old and full form of this deed, see page 210.

Episcopal Church, according to the true intent and meaning of the following form of a deed of settlement: anything in the said form to the contrary notwithstanding.

THIS INDENTURE, made this day of in the year of our Lord one thousand hundred and between of the in the State of (if the grantor be married, insert the name of his wife) of the one part, and trustees, in trust for the use and purposes herein after mentioned, all of the in the State of aforesaid, of the other part, WITNESSETH, that the said (if married, insert the name of his wife,) for and in consideration of the sum of specie, to in hand paid, at and upon the sealing and delivery of these presents, the receipt whereof is hereby acknowledged, hath (or have) given, granted, bargained, sold, released, confirmed, and conveyed, and by these presents doth (or do) give, grant, bargain, sell, release, confirm, and convey unto them the said and their successors, (trustees, in trust for the uses and purposes herein after mentioned and declared,) all the estate, right, title, interest, property, claim, and demand whatsoever, either in law or equity, which he the said (if married, here insert the name of his wife) hath (or have) in, to, or upon all and singular a certain lot, or piece of land, situate, lying, and being in the and State aforesaid, bounded and butted as follows, to wit, (here insert the several courses and distances of the land to the place of beginning,) containing and laid out for acres of land, together with all and singular the houses, woods, waters, ways, privileges, and appurtenances thereto belonging, or in anywise pertaining: TO HAVE AND TO HOLD all and singular, the above-mentioned and described lot or piece of land, situate, lying, and being as aforesaid, together with all and singular the houses, woods, waters, ways, and privileges thereto belonging, or in anywise appertaining unto them the said and their successors in office forever in trust, that they shall erect and build, or cause to be erected and built thereon, a house or place of worship for the use of the members of the Methodist Episcopal Church in the United States of America, according to the rules and discipline which from time to time may be agreed upon and adopted by the ministers and preachers of the said Church at their General Conferences in the United States of America; and in further trust and confidence that they shall at all times, forever hereafter, permit such ministers and preachers belonging to the said Church, as shall from time to time be duly authorized by the General Conferences of the ministers and preachers of the said Methodist Episcopal Church, or by the Annual Conferences authorized by the said General Conference, to preach and expound God's holy word therein; And the said doth by these presents warrant, and forever defend, all and singular the before-mentioned and described lot or piece of land with the appurtenances thereto belonging unto them the said and their successors, chosen and appointed as aforesaid, from the claim or claims of him the said his heirs and assigns, and from the claim or claims of all persons whatever. In testimony whereof, the said (if married, insert the name of his wife) have hereto set their hands and seals, the day and year aforesaid.

Sealed and delivered in the presence of us (Two witnesses.)

Grantor's (L. S.)
his wife's (L. S.)

Received the day of the date of the above-written indenture, the consideration therein mentioned in full.

Witness.] Grantor's (L. S.)

County, ss.

Be it remembered, that on the day of in the year of our Lord one thousand personally appeared before me, one of the justices of the peace, in and for the county of and State of the within-named the grantor (if married, insert the name of his wife) acknowledged the within deed of trust to be their act and deed, for the uses and purposes therein mentioned and declared; and she the said wife of the said being separate and apart from her said husband, by me examined, declared that she had made the same acknowledgment, freely and with her own consent, without being induced thereto through fear or threats of her said husband. In testimony whereof I have hereto set my hand and seal, the day and year first above written.

Here the justice's name. (L. S.)

SECTION III.

Of Trustees.

1. Let nine trustees be appointed for holding church property, where proper persons can be procured; otherwise seven or five.

2. When a new board of trustees is to be created, it shall be done (except in those States and Territories where the statutes provide differently) by the appointment of the preacher in charge, or the Presiding Elder of the district.

3. When any one or more of the trustees shall die, or cease to be a member or members of the said Church according to the rules of the discipline as aforesaid, then and in such case it shall be the duty of the stationed minister or preacher (authorized as aforesaid) who shall have the pastoral charge of the members of the said Church, (except in those States and Territories where

the statutes provide differently,) to call a meeting of the remaining trustees as soon as conveniently may be: and when so met, the said minister or preacher shall proceed to nominate one or more persons to fill the place or places of him or them whose office [or offices] has [or have] been vacated as aforesaid. *Provided*, the person or persons so nominated shall have been one year a member or members of the said Church immediately preceding such nomination, and be at least twenty-one years of age; and the said trustees, so assembled, shall proceed to elect, and by a majority of votes appoint, the person or persons so nominated to fill such vacancy or vacancies, in order to keep up the number of nine trustees forever; and in case of an equal number of votes for and against the said nomination, the stationed minister or preacher shall have the casting vote.

Provided nevertheless, That if the said trustees, or any of them, or their successors, have advanced, or shall advance, any sum or sums of money, or are or shall be responsible for any sum or sums of money, on account of the said premises, and they the said trustees, or their successors, be obliged to pay the said sums of money, they, or a majority of them, shall be authorized to raise the said sum or sums of money by a mortgage on the said premises, or by selling the said premises, after notice given to the pastor or preacher who has the oversight of the congregation attending divine service on the said premises, if the money due be not paid to the said trustees, or their successors, within one year after such notice given; and if such sale take place, the said trustees, or their successors, after paying the debt and other expenses which are due from the money arising from such sale, shall deposit the remainder of the money produced by the said sale in the hands of the Steward or Stewards of the society belonging to or attending divine service on said premises: which surplus of the produce of such sale, so deposited in the hands of the said Steward or Stewards, shall be at the disposal of the next Annual Conference authorized as aforesaid; which said Annual Conference shall dispose of the said money, according to the best of their judgment, for the use of the said society.

4. No person shall be eligible as a trustee to any of our houses, churches, or schools, who is not a regular member of our Church.

5. No person who is a trustee shall be ejected while he is in joint security for money, unless such relief be given him as is demanded, or the creditor will accept.

6. The Board of Trustees of every circuit or station shall be responsible to the Quarterly Conference of said circuit or station, and shall be required to present a report of its acts during the preceding year.

CHAPTER III.

OF SUPPORT AND SUPPLIES.

SECTION I.

Of the Support of Bishops.

Quest. WHAT shall be allowed for the support of a Bishop, and how shall it be raised?

Answ. 1. The annual allowance of a married Bishop shall be two hundred dollars, and his travelling expenses. The annual allowance of an unmarried bishop shall be one hundred dollars, and his travelling expenses.

2. Each child of a Bishop shall be allowed sixteen dollars annually to the age of seven years, and twenty-four dollars annually from the age of seven to fourteen years.

3. Each Annual Conference shall pay its proportionate part toward the allowance of the widows and orphans of Bishops.

4. Each Annual Conference in which a Bishop or Bishops may reside, shall annually appoint a committee of three or more, whose duty it shall be to estimate the amount necessary to furnish a house, fuel, and table expenses, for said Bishop or Bishops, subject to the action of the Conference, and they are authorized to draw on the funds of the Book Concern for said amount; and also for the amount of their quarterage and travelling expenses.

SECTION II.

Of the Allowance to the Ministers and Preachers, and to their Wives, Widows, and Children.

1. The annual allowance of the married travelling, supernumerary, and superannuated preachers, shall be two hundred dollars, and their travelling expenses.

2 The annual allowance of the unmarried travelling, supernumerary, and superannuated preachers, shall be one hundred dollars, and their travelling expenses.

3. Each child of a travelling preacher shall be allowed sixteen dollars annually, to the age of seven years, and twenty-four dollars annually from the age of seven to fourteen years; and those preachers whose wives are dead shall be allowed for each child annually a sum sufficient to pay the board of such child or children during the above term of years: *Nevertheless*, this rule shall not apply to the children of preachers whose families are provided for by other means in their circuits respectively.

4. The annual allowance of the widows of travelling, superannuated, worn-out, and supernumerary preachers, and the Bishops, shall be one hundred dollars.

5. The orphans of travelling, supernumerary, superannuated, and worn-out preachers, and the Bishops, shall be allowed by the Annual Conferences, the same sums respect-

ively which are allowed to the children of living preachers. And on the death of a preacher leaving a child or children without so much of worldly goods as should be necessary to his, her, or their support, the Annual Conference of which he was a member shall raise, in such manner as may be deemed best, a yearly sum for the subsistence and education of such orphan child or children, until he, she, or they, shall have arrived at fourteen years of age. The amount of which yearly sum shall be fixed by a committee of the Conference at each session in advance.

6. It shall be the duty of a committee appointed by the Quarterly Conference, who shall be members of our Church, to make an estimate of the amount necessary to furnish fuel and table expenses for the family or families of preachers stationed with them, which estimate shall be subject to the action of the Quarterly Conference; and the Stewards shall provide, by such means as they may devise, to meet such expenses, in money or otherwise: *provided* the Stewards shall not appropriate the moneys collected for the regular quarterly allowance of the preachers to the payment of family expenses.

Quest. How shall the Presiding Elders be supported?

Answ. 1. If there be a surplus of the public money in one or more circuits in his district, he shall receive such surplus; *provided* he do not receive more than his an nual allowance. In case of a deficiency in his allowance, after such surplus is paid him, or if there be no surplus, he shall share with the preachers of his district in proportion with what they have respectively received, so that he receives no more than the amount of his allowance upon the whole: he shall be accountable to the Annual Conference for what he receives as his allowance.

2. There shall be a meeting in every district, of one Steward from each station and circuit, to be selected from among the Stewards by the Quarterly Conference, whose duty it shall be, by and with the advice of the Presiding Elder, (who shall preside in such meeting,) to take into consideration the general state of the district in regard to temporalities, and to furnish a house, fuel, and table expenses, for the Presiding Elder, and to apportion his entire claim among the different circuits and stations in the district according to their several ability.

The more effectually to raise the amount necessary to meet the above-mentioned allowances, let there be made weekly class collections in all our societies where it is practicable: and also for the support of missions and missionary schools under our care.

If the above allowances are not raised as provided for, the Church shall not be accountable for the deficiency, as in a case of debt.

SECTION III.

Local Preachers to have an Allowance in certain Cases.

1. Whenever a local preacher fills the place of a travelling preacher by the approbation of the Presiding Elder, he shall be paid for his time a sum proportional to the allowance of a travelling preacher; which sum shall be paid by the circuit at the next quarterly meeting, if the travelling preacher whose place he filled up were either sick or necessarily absent: or, in other cases, out of the allowance of the travelling preacher.

2. If a local preacher be distressed in his temporal circumstances, on account of his service in the circuit, he may apply to the Quarterly Conference, who may give him what relief they judge proper, after the allowance of the travelling preachers and of their wives, and all other regular allowances, are discharged.

SECTION IV.

Of the Qualifications, Appointment, and Duty, of the Stewards of Circuits and Stations.

Quest. 1. What are the qualifications necessary for Stewards?

Answ. Let them be men of solid piety, who both know and love the Methodist doctrine and discipline, and of good natural and acquired abilities to transact the temporal business.

Quest. 2. How are the Stewards to be appointed?

Answ. The preacher having the charge of the circuit shall have the right of nomination; but the Quarterly Conference shall confirm or reject such nomination.

Quest. 3. What are the duties of Stewards?

Answ. To take an exact account of all the money or other provisions collected for the support of preachers in the circuit; to make an accurate return of every expenditure of money, whether to the preachers, the sick, or the poor; to seek the needy and distressed in order to relieve and comfort them; to inform the preachers of any sick or disorderly persons; to tell the preachers what they think wrong in them; to attend the quarterly meetings of their circuit; to give advice, if asked, in planning the circuit; to attend committees for the application of money to Churches; to give counsel in matters of arbitration; provide elements for the Lord's supper; to write circular letters to the societies in the circuit to be more liberal if need be; as also to let them know, when occasion requires, the state of the temporal concerns at the last quarterly meeting; to register the marriages and baptisms; and to be subject to the Bishops, the Presiding Elder of their district, and the Elder, Deacon, and travelling preachers of their circuit. (See also § 5, art. 2, p. 184, and § 6, answ. 2, page 189.)

Quest. 4. To whom are the Stewards accountable for the faithful performance of their duty?

Answ. To the Quarterly Conference of the circuit or station, which shall have power to dismiss or change them at pleasure.

Quest. 5. What number of Stewards are necessary in each circuit?

Answ. Not less than three, nor more than seven, one of whom shall be the Recording Steward.

SECTION V.

Of raising Annual Supplies for the Propagation of the Gospel, making up the Allowance of the Preachers, &c.

1. Every preacher who has the charge of a circuit shall earnestly recommend to every class or society in his circuit to raise a quarterly or annual collection by voluntary contribution, or in such other way or manner as they may judge most expedient from time to time; and the moneys so collected shall be lodged with the Steward or Stewards of the circuit, to be brought or sent to the Annual Conference, with a regular account of the sums raised for this purpose in the classes or societies respectively.

2. Wherever there remains in the hands of the Stewards a surplus of the moneys raised for the use of the circuit preachers, after paying the allowance of the preachers in the circuit, let such surplus be brought or sent to the Annual Conference.

3. Every preacher who has the charge of

a circuit shall make a yearly collection, and, if expedient, a quarterly one, in every congregation where there is a probability that the people will be willing to contribute; and the money so collected shall be lodged in the hands of the Steward or Stewards, and brought or sent to the ensuing Annual Conference. To this end, he may read and enlarge upon the following hints:—

"How shall we send labourers into those parts where they are most of all wanted? Many are willing to hear, but not to bear the expense. Nor can it as yet be expected of them. Stay till the word of God has touched their hearts, and then they will gladly provide for them that preach it. Does it not lie upon us, in the mean time, to supply their lack of service? To raise money out of which, from time to time, that expense may be defrayed? By this means, those who willingly offer themselves may travel through every part, whether there be societies or not, and stay wherever there is a call, without being burdensome to any. Thus may the gospel, in the life and power thereof, be spread from sea to sea. Which of you will not rejoice to throw in your mite to promote this glorious work?

"Besides this, in carrying on so large a work through the continent, there are calls for money in various ways, and we must frequently be at a considerable expense, or the work must be at a full stop. Many, too, are the *occasional* distresses of our preachers, or their families, which require an immediate supply, otherwise their hands would hang down, if they were not constrained to depart from the work.

"The money contributed will be brought to the ensuing Conference.

"Men and brethren, help! Was there ever a call like this since you first heard the gospel sound? Help to relieve your companions in the kingdom of Jesus, who are pressed above measure. Bear ye one another's burdens, and so fulfil the law of Christ. Help to send forth able and willing labourers into your Lord's harvest: so shall ye be assistants in saving souls from death, and hiding a multitude of sins. Help to propagate the gospel of your salvation to the remotest corners of the earth, till the knowledge of our Lord shall cover the land as the waters cover the sea. So shall it appear to ourselves and all men, that we are indeed one body, united by one spirit; so shall the baptized heathens be yet again constrained to say, 'See how these Christians love one another!'"

4. A public collection shall be made at every Annual and every General Conference, for the above purposes.

5. Let the annual produce of the Charter Fund, as divided among the several Conferences, be applied with the above contributions: but so as not to militate against the rules of the Charter Fund; and also the annual dividend arising from the profits of the Book Concern. Out of the moneys so collected, and brought to the respective An-

nual Conferences, let the various allowances agreed upon in the second section be made up; but each Annual Conference shall have full power to determine, by a vote of two-thirds of all the members present and voting, who among the superannuated and supernumerary preachers, and the widows and orphans of deceased preachers belonging to the Conference, shall be claimants on the funds of said Conference, and what amount each claimant shall receive from year to year. But in no case shall an allowance be made to any travelling preacher who has travelled in any circuit where he might, in the judgment of the Annual Conference, have obtained his full quarterage, if he had applied for it; and if at any Conference their remain a surplus after making up all such allowances, the Conference shall send such surplus forward to that Conference they judge to be the most necessitous.

6. Every Annual Conference has full liberty to adopt and recommend such plans and rules as to them may appear necessary the more effectually to raise supplies for the respective allowances. Each Annual Conference is authorized to raise a fund, if they judge it proper, subject to its own control, and under such regulations as their wisdom may direct, for the relief of the distressed travelling, superannuated, and supernumerary preachers, their wives, widows, and children, as also for missionary purposes.

7. It shall be the duty of each Annual Conference to take measures, from year to

year, to raise moneys in every circuit and station within its bounds, for the relief of its necessitous superannuated and supernumerary ministers, widows, and orphans. And the Conference shall annually appoint a committee to estimate the several sums necessary to be allowed for the extra expenses of such necessitous claimants, who shall be paid in proportion to the estimates made and the moneys in hand.

8. To defray the expenses of the delegates composing the General Conference, a collection shall be taken up in each circuit and station some time previously to the sitting of the Conference, and the sums so collected shall be brought up to the General Conference, and applied to the object herein contemplated in proportion to the expenses of the several delegates.

SECTION VI.

Of Building and Renting Houses for the Use of the Travelling Preachers.

Quest. What advice or direction shall be given concerning the building or renting of dwelling-houses for the use of the married travelling preachers?

Answ. 1. It is recommended by the General Conference to the travelling preachers, to advise our friends in general to purchase a lot of ground in each circuit, and to build a preacher's house thereon, and to furnish it with, at least, heavy furniture, and to settle the same on trustees appointed by the Quarterly Conference, according to the Deed of Settlement published in our form of Discipline.

2. The General Conference recommend to all the circuits, in cases where they are not able to comply with the above request, to rent a house for the married preacher and his family, (when such are stationed upon their circuits respectively) and that the Annual Conferences do assist to make up the rents of such houses as far as they can, when the circuit cannot do it.

The Stewards of each circuit and station shall be a standing committee, (where no trustees are constituted for that purpose,) to provide houses for the families of our married preachers, or to assist the preachers to obtain houses for themselves when they are appointed to labour among them.

3. It shall be the duty of the Presiding Elders and preachers to use their influence to carry the above rules respecting building and renting houses for the accommodation of preachers and their families into effect In order to this, each Quarterly Conference shall appoint a committee, (unless other measures have been adopted,) who, with the advice and aid of the preachers and Presiding Elders, shall devise such means as may seem fit to raise moneys for that purpose. And it is recommended to the Annual Conferences to make a special inquiry of their members respecting this part of their duty.

4. Those preachers who refuse to occupy the houses which may be provided for them on the stations and circuits where they are from time to time appointed, shall be allowed nothing for house rent, nor receive anything more than quarterage for themselves, their wives, and children, and their travelling expenses. *Nevertheless*, this rule shall not apply to those preachers whose families are either established within the bounds of their circuits, or are so situated that in the judgment of the Stewards, or the above-mentioned committee, it is not necessary, for the benefit of the circuit, to remove them.

CHAPTER IV.

THE SUPPORT OF MISSIONS.

1. The support of missions is committed to the Churches, congregations, and societies, as such.

2. It shall be the duty of each Annual Conference, where missions have been or are to be established, to appoint a standing committee, (which shall keep a record of its doings, and report the same to its Conference,) whose duty it shall be, in conjunction with the President of the Conference, to make an estimate of the amount necessary for the support of each mission and mission school, in addition to the regular allowance of the Discipline to preachers and their

families from year to year: for which amount the President of the Conference for the time being shall draw on the Treasurer of the Society in quarterly instalments.

3. It shall be the duty of each Annual Conference to form within its bounds a Conference Missionary Society, which shall appoint its own officers, fix the terms of membership, and otherwise regulate its own administration. But it shall pay all its funds into the treasury of the parent society.

4. It shall be the duty of each Presiding Elder to bring the subject of our missions before the Quarterly Conference of each circuit and station within his district, at the first Quarterly Conference in each year; and said Conference shall proceed to appoint a committee, of not less than *three* nor more than *nine*, (of which the preacher in charge shall be chairman,) to be called the Committee on Missions, whose duty it shall be to aid the preacher in charge in carrying into effect the disciplinary measures for the support of our missions.

5. It shall be the duty of the preacher in charge, aided by the Committee on Missions, to provide for the diffusion of missionary intelligence in the Church and congregation.

6. It shall be the duty of the preacher in charge, aided by the Committee on Missions, to institute a monthly missionary prayer-meeting, or lecture, in each society, or

Church and congregation, wherever practicable, for the purpose of imploring the divine blessing on missions; for the diffusion of missionary intelligence; and to afford an opportunity for voluntary offerings to the missionary cause.

7. It shall be the duty of the preacher in charge, aided by the Committee on Missions, to appoint missionary collectors, and furnish them with suitable books and instructions, that they may call on each member of the society, or Church and congregation, and on other persons, at their discretion, for his or her annual, semi-annual, quarterly, monthly, or weekly contributions for the support of missions. Said collectors shall make monthly returns (unless otherwise instructed by the committee) to the preacher in charge, or to the Missionary Treasurer of the Church, if there be such treasurer appointed by the Committee on Missions. Such returns shall be fairly entered in a book, which the committee shall provide, together with collections and contributions received from other sources. Such entries shall set forth the name of each collector, the real or assumed names of the contributors to each collector, with the amount contributed by each.

8. Each preacher in charge shall report at Conference, to the Executive Committee, or Board of Managers of the Conference Missionary Society, a plain transcript of the record of the returns provided for in section seven, comprehending the name of each

collector in his charge, and the name, real or assumed, of each contributor to each collector of *fifty cents* or upwards during the year; and the aggregate sum of all contributions under *fifty* cents each, that they may be by said Executive Committee, or Board of Managers, properly arranged by districts, and by charges, for publication in the Annual Report of the Conference Missionary Society; together with the contributions and collections received from other sources, unless the Conference shall by vote declare such transcript returns, and such publication, not to be advisable.

9. It shall be the duty of the preacher in charge, with the aid of the Committee on Missions, to present once in the year, to the Societies, or the Churches and congregations, the cause of missions, and to ask public collections and contributions for the support of the same. The manner of asking and taking such collections and contributions shall be at the discretion of the pastor and the Committee on Missions, with this injunction, that the pastor shall preach, or cause to be preached on the occasion, one or more sermons: and with the recommendation that one whole Sabbath day be given to the cause, on this annual presentation of missions, in our principal Churches and congregations.

10. It is earnestly recommended that each Sunday school in our Churches and congregations be organized into a Missionary Society, under such rules and regulations as

the pastor, the superintendent, and teachers may prescribe.

11. Each Annual Conference shall designate the month or months in which the public collections and contributions for missions shall be taken within its bounds.

12. The President of the Conference, at each session, shall appoint one of its members, with an alternate, to preach a missionary sermon during its next succeeding session, at such time and place as the officers of the Conference Missionary Society shall designate, and said officers shall cause timely notice of such sermon to be published abroad.

13. It will be expected in the examination in the Annual Conference, reference will be had to the faithful performance of the duty of preachers on this subject in the passage of character.

14. Each Presiding Elder is charged with seeing that the foregoing provisions, so far as applicable to his district, are faithfully executed within his district.

15. The Corresponding Secretary of the Missionary Society of the Methodist Episcopal Church shall be a member of such Annual Conference as he may, with the approbation of the Bishops, select.

16. Any Annual Conference may, at its option, by a vote of two-thirds of its members, assume the responsibility of supporting such missions, already established within its own limits, as have hitherto been reported under the head of "Missions in the Destitute Por-

tions of the Regular Work;" and for this purpose it shall be at liberty to organize a Conference Domestic Society, with branches; *provided* such organization shall not interfere with the collections for the Missionary Society of the Methodist Episcopal Church, as required by the Discipline. *Provided, also,* that in case more funds shall be raised for such missions than are needed, the surplus shall be paid over to the Treasurer of the Parent Society of the Methodist Episcopal Church, at New-York, to be appropriated to such mission or missions, under the care of the Society, as may be designated by said Conference.

CHAPTER V.

OF THE CHARTERED FUND.

Quest. 1. WHAT further provision shall be made for the distressed travelling preachers, for the families of travelling preachers, and for the superannuated and worn-out preachers, and the widows and orphans of preachers?

Answ. There shall be a Chartered Fund, to be supported by the voluntary contributions of our friends: the principal stock of which shall be funded under the direction of trustees, chosen by the General Conference, and the interest applied under the direction of the General Conference, according to the following regulations, namely:—

1. The Elders, and those who have the

oversight of circuits, shall be collectors and receivers of subscriptions, &c., for this fund.

2. The money shall, if possible, be conveyed by bills of exchange, or otherwise, through the means of the post, to the general Book Agents, who shall pay it to the trustees of the fund: otherwise, it shall be brought to the ensuing Annual Conference.

3. The interest shall be divided into thirty-eight parts, and each of the Annual Conferences shall have authority to draw one thirty-eighth part out of the fund; and if in one or more Conferences a part less than one thirty-eighth be drawn out of the fund in any given year, then in such case or cases, the other Annual Conferences, held in the same year, shall have authority, if they judge it necessary, to draw out of the fund such surplus of the interest which has not been applied by the former Conferences; and the Bishops shall bring the necessary information of the state of the interest of the fund, respecting the year in question, from Conference to Conference.

4. All drafts on the Chartered Fund shall be made on the President of the said fund, by order of the Annual Conference, signed by the President, and countersigned by the Secretary of the said Conference.

5. The money subscribed for the Chartered Fund may be lodged, on proper securities, in the States respectively in which it has been subscribed, under the direction of deputies living in such States respectively; *provided*, such securities and such deputies

be proposed as shall be approved of by the trustees in Philadelphia; and the stock in which it is proposed to lodge the money be sufficiently productive to give satisfaction to the trustees.

Quest. 2. How shall vacancies in the board of trustees of the Chartered Fund be filled?

Answ. The Board of Trustees shall have power to fill any vacancy or vacancies that may occur in their body by death, resignation, or otherwise, subject, however, to the approval of the first General Conference that may be held after such vacancy or vacancies shall have occurred.

CHAPTER VI.

PRINTING AND CIRCULATING OF BOOKS, TRACTS, AND PERIODICALS.

1. THE principal establishment of the Book Concern shall be in the city of New-York; and there shall be such other establishments as the General Conference may deem expedient.

2. There shall be an Editor of the Methodist Quarterly Review and general books, and an Editor for the Christian Advocate and Journal, who, if chosen from among the travelling preachers, shall be members of such Conferences as they may, with the approbation of the Bishop, select. There shall be an Editor at New-York of Sunday-school publications, whose duty it shall be,

in connexion with the Book Agents, to superintend all such publications issued at our Book Room, and to have charge of the Sunday School Advocate or other Sunday-school periodicals, and he shall be subject to the same regulations and restrictions which govern the other Editors in New-York. The Editor of Sunday-school publications shall also be the Corresponding Secretary of our Sunday-School Union.

3. There shall be at New York an Editor of a Monthly Magazine and of Tracts, who shall be subject to the same regulations and restrictions which govern other Editors at New-York, and who shall also be the Corresponding Secretary of our Tract Society: as Editor of Tracts, he shall have charge of the publication of tracts in our own and foreign languages; as Corresponding Secretary of the Tract Society, it shall be his duty to raise funds in behalf of the Society, to promote the formation of Conference and other auxiliaries, to co-operate with the auxiliary societies, to make all proper efforts for the general diffusion of religious reading, and to make arrangements with the Book Agents for the cheap publication of any book or books, specially adapted to promote evangelical and practical religion.

4. There shall be an Agent and an Assistant Agent, both of whom shall be chosen from among the travelling preachers, and shall be members of such Conferences as they may, with the approbation of the Bishops, select.

5. The Agents shall have authority to regulate the publications and all other parts of the business of the Concern, except what belongs to the editorial departments, as the state of the finances will admit, and the demands may require. It shall be their duty to send an exhibit of the state of the Book Concern at New-York to each session of the Annual Conferences, and report quadrennially to the General Conference. They shall also inform the Conferences of any within their respective bounds who neglect to make payment, that measures may be taken to collect or secure such debts; and they shall not allow any claim to run beyond one year from the time it was due without reporting it to the Conference. They shall publish such books and tracts as are recommended by the General Conference, and may, if approved by the Editors, publish such as are recommended by the Book Committee at New-York, or recommended by an Annual Conference; and they may reprint any book or tract which has been once approved and published by us, when in their judgment, and in the judgment of the Editors, the same ought to be reprinted; or they may publish any new work which may be approved by the Editors.

6. The Book Committee at New-York shall consist of seven travelling ministers, to be chosen by the General Conference. During the intervals of the General Conference, they shall have power to fill any vacancy that may occur in their own body. It shall

be the duty of the Book Committee to examine into the condition of the Book Concern, to inspect the accounts of the Agents, and make a report thereof yearly to all the Annual Conferences, and to the General Conference. They shall also attend to such matters as may be referred to them by the Editors or Agents for their action or counsel. And they shall have power to suspend an Editor or Agent from his official relation as such, if they judge it necessary for the interests of the Church and the Concern. And a time shall be fixed, at as early a day as practicable, for the investigation of the official conduct of the said Editor or Agent, at which two or more of the Bishops shall be requested to attend; and by the concurrence of the Bishops present, and of the majority of the Committee, he may be removed from office in the interval of the General Conference. And in case a vacancy occurs in any of the agencies or editorial departments authorized by the General Conference, it shall be the duty of the Book Committee, and two or more of the General Superintendents, as soon as practicable, to provide for such vacancy until the next General Conference.

7. There shall be an Agent and an Assistant Agent to conduct the Book Concern in Cincinnati, to be chosen from among the travelling preachers, who shall manage the business in the western country, so as to co-operate with the Agents at New-York, and shall be members of such Conferences as

they may, with the approbation of the Bishops, select.

(1.) They shall have authority to publish any book or tract which has been previously published by the Agents at New-York, when in their judgment, and in the judgment of the Book Committee, the demand for such publication will justify, and the interests of the Church require it. *Provided*, they shall not reprint our large works, such as the Commentaries, quarto Bible, Wesley's and Fletcher's Works, or any other work containing more than seven hundred pages. And the Agents at New-York shall fill the orders for the Agents at Cincinnati for the plates of such books or tracts; and when the Agents at New-York are about to issue any new work of less than seven hundred pages, they shall, when practicable, give notice to the Agents at Cincinnati, and furnish, if ordered by them, duplicate plates, which, with the above, shall be at cost.

(2.) They shall publish such books and tracts as are recommended to them for publication by the General Conference; and they may publish any new work which shall be approved by the Editors; and may publish any work recommended by the Book Committee at Cincinnati, or by an Annual Conference, if approved by the Editors.

(3.) Printed sheets ordered by the Agents from New-York shall be sent at fifty per cent., and bound books of the General Catalogue at forty per cent., discount from the retail prices; and those ordered from Cincinnati to New-York to be sent on the same terms, the agency sending the books to be charged with the expense of transportation.

(4.) It shall be the duty of the Agents to send an exhibit of the state of the Book Concern at Cincinnati to each session of all the Annual Conferences, and report quadrennially to the General Conference. They shall also inform the Conferences of any within their respective bounds who neglect to make payment, that measures may be taken to collect or secure such debts; and they shall not allow any claim to run beyond one year from the time it was due without reporting it to the Conference.

(5.) The Book Committee of this department of the Book Concern shall consist of seven travelling ministers, to be chosen by the General Conference, whose powers and duties in reference to this establishment shall be the same as those of the Book Committee at New-York in relation to the Concern there.

(6.) The Agents of this establishment shall remit to the Agents at New-York during the current year as largely and frequently as their funds will allow, and to the full amount of stock furnished, if practicable. They shall also remit any surplus funds that may be in their hands after defraying the expense of conducting their business, which shall be added to the profits of the Concern at New-York, and appropriated to the same purposes.

(7.) There shall be an Editor of the Ladies'

Repository, general books and tracts, except those in the German language, and an Editor of the Western Christian Advocate, who, if chosen from among the travelling preachers, shall be members of such Conferences as they may, with the approbation of the Bishops, select.

(8.) There shall be an Editor in the German department, who shall have charge of the Christian Apologist, and perform all the editorial duties necessary in the printing of such books and tracts as may be recommended to the agents as above, for publication in the German language.

8. Every Annual Conference shall appoint a committee, who, in the absence of the Agent, shall attend to the collection of the accounts sent out from the Book Concern, and return an accurate report of the same. They shall also report to the Conference any claims which may have been one year due, that they may be collected or secured. Every Presiding Elder, minister, and preacher, shall do everything in his power to recover all debts due to the Concern, for books or periodicals, within the bounds of his charge. If any person, preacher, or member, be indebted to the Book Concern, and refuse or neglect to make payment, or to come to a just settlement, let him be dealt with in the same manner as is directed in other cases of debt and disputed accounts. (See part i, chap. ix, sec. 4.)

9. Whenever a member of an Annual Conference applies for a location, it shall be

asked in all cases, Is he indebted to the Book Concern? and if it be ascertained that he is, the Conference shall require him to secure said debt, if they judge it at all necessary or proper, before they grant him a location. Whenever any claimant on the funds of a Conference shall be in debt to the Book Concern, the Conference of which he is a member shall have power to appropriate the amount of such claim, or any part thereof, to the payment of said debt.

10. In addition to the Christian Advocate and Journal, and the Western Christian Advocate, there shall be similar papers established in Pittsburgh, Pa.; Auburn, New-York; Chicago, Ill.; St. Louis, Mo., (when the agents at Cincinnati deem it advisable;) and San Francisco, California. The Pittsburgh Conference shall appoint from their own members a Publishing Committee, consisting of three, whose duties shall be similar to those of the Book Committees of New-York and Cincinnati, so far as they may be applicable to the Pittsburgh Christian Advocate. In the case of the Northern Christian Advocate, the Publishing Committee shall be appointed by the Oneida, Genesee, East Genesee, Black River, and Wyoming Conferences, and shall consist of one member from each of these Conferences, to be chosen annually. There shall be a Publishing Committee for the North-Western Christian Advocate, consisting of one member from each of the following Conferences,

to be selected by the Conferences respectively; namely, Rock River, Michigan, North-Western Indiana, Illinois, Iowa, and Wisconsin; whose duty shall be similar to that of the Book Committee at New-York and Cincinnati, so far as it may be applicable to the establishment. A committee of one from the Illinois, one from the Southern Illinois, one from the Iowa, one from the Arkansas, and one from the Missouri Conferences, to be selected by the Conferences respectively, shall superintend the publication of the paper authorized to be published at St. Louis, Mo.; and on the nomination of said committee and recommendation of the Missouri Conference, the Presiding Bishop shall be requested to appoint an editor for said paper, when the Book Agents at Cincinnati shall have determined on its publication; and the duties of said committee shall be similar to those of the Publishing Committee at Chicago. There shall be a Publishing Committee, consisting of four members, to be selected by the California, and one by the Oregon Annual Conference, whose duties shall be similar to the Book Committees at New-York and Cincinnati, so far as they may be applicable to the California Christian Advocate.

11. The editors of the papers at Pittsburgh, Auburn, Chicago, and San Francisco, shall be elected by the General Conference. And in case of vacancy by death, resignation, or otherwise, in either of these establishments, the Annual Conference where it is located

shall have authority to fill such vacancy as above provided.

12. The Publishing Committee in each of these establishments shall keep an account of the receipts and expenditures for the paper, correspond with the agents at New-York, hold all moneys, after defraying current expenses, subject to their order, and shall report annually on the state of the establishment to their Conference, and to the agents at New-York. And whenever it shall be found that such papers do not fully support themselves, it shall be the duty of the Annual Conferences within whose bounds they are established, to discontinue them, and report to the agents at New-York the state of the accounts on the final settlement of the business; and if there be any loss, the said agents shall take the earliest opportunity to discharge the debt.

13. The Annual Conferences are affectionately and earnestly requested not to establish any more Conference papers; and where such papers exist, they may be discontinued when it can be done consistently with existing obligations.

14. There shall be a depository of our books at Pittsburgh, Pa.; at Boston, Mass.; and at San Francisco, Cal., furnished by the agents at New-York with full supplies of the books of our General Catalogue, Sunday-school books and tracts, to be sold for the Concern on the same terms as at New-York. *Provided*, that there shall not be more than fifteen thousand dollars' worth at Pittsburgh,

nor more than ten thousand dollars' worth at Boston. There shall also be a depository at Chicago, Ill., and one at St. Louis, Mo., to be supplied by the agents at Cincinnati. Depositories shall also be established at Buffalo and Auburn, N. Y., and at Washington, D. C., at the discretion of the New-York Book Agents.

15. The expenses incident to the transportation, management, and sale of our books at these depositories, having been met out of the sales according to an arrangement with the agents at New-York, the net proceeds shall be forwarded to said agents as fast as possible.

16. Full statements shall be made to the agents at New-York semi-annually, at dates fixed by them, of the amount of sales, and of expenses; distinguishing cash sales from those on credit. And also, annual statements shall be made of the amount of stock.

17. If it shall appear to the agents at New-York that the business at either of the depositories is not well managed, or that remittances are not duly made, they shall give notice thereof to the committee or commissioners acting for the Annual Conference, or to the Annual Conference, who shall immediately correct the error complained of, or cause the affairs of the depository to be wound up.

18. The salaries for the support of editors and agents in all our book and periodical establishments, shall be fixed by the General

Conference, or by committees appointed by that body.

19. No books shall *hereafter* be issued on commission, either from New-York, Cincinnati, or any other depository or establishment under our direction.

20. The profits arising from the Book Concern, after a sufficient capital to carry on the business is retained, shall be regularly applied to the support of the deficient travelling preachers and their families, the widows and orphans of preachers, &c. The Book Agents shall every year send forward to each Annual Conference an account of the dividend which the several Annual Conferences may draw that year: and each Conference may draw for its proportionate part on any person who has book money in hands, and the drafts, with the receipt of the Conference thereon, shall be sent to the Book Agents, and be placed to the credit of the person who paid the same.

21. Any travelling preacher who may publish any work or book of his own, shall be responsible to his Conference for any obnoxious matter or doctrine therein contained.

22. No editor, agent, or clerk, employed in the Book Concern, or in any department belonging to it, shall be allowed in any case to publish or sell books as his own private property.

CHAPTER VII.

OF SLAVERY.

Quest. WHAT shall be done for the extirpation of the evil of slavery?

Answ. 1. We declare that we are as much as ever convinced of the great evil of slavery: therefore no slaveholder shall be eligible to any official station in our Church hereafter, where the laws of the State in which he lives will admit of emancipation, and permit the liberated slave to enjoy freedom.

2. When any travelling preacher becomes an owner of a slave or slaves, by any means, he shall forfeit his ministerial character in our Church, unless he execute, if it be practicable, a legal emancipation of such slaves, conformably to the laws of the State in which he lives.

3. All our preachers shall prudently enforce upon our members the necessity of teaching their slaves to read the word of God; and to allow them time to attend upon the public worship of God on our regular days of divine service.

4. Our coloured preachers and official members shall have all the privileges which are usual to others in the district and Quarterly Conferences, where the usages of the country do not forbid it. And the Presiding Elder may hold for them a separate District Conference, where the number of coloured local preachers will justify it.

5. The Bishops may employ coloured preachers to travel and preach, when their services are judged necessary, *provided* that no one shall be so employed without having been recommended by a Quarterly Conference.

⁂ NOTE.—The phrase, "wherever practicable," at the top of page 170, though authorized by the recorded Journal of the General Conference of 1852, is believed by many of the Delegates to be without authority.

FORM OF A DEED OF SETTLEMENT.

Quest. 4. WHAT shall be done for the security of our preaching-houses, and the premises belonging thereto?

Answ Let the following plan of a deed of settlement be brought into effect in all possible cases, and as far as the laws of the states respectively will admit of it. But each annual conference is authorized to make such modification in the deeds as they may find the different usages and customs of law require in the different states and territories, so as to secure the premises firmly by deed, and permanently to the Methodist Episcopal Church, according to the true intent and meaning of the following form of a deed of settlement; anything in the said form to the contrary notwithstanding.

THIS INDENTURE, made this day of in the year of our Lord one thousand hundred and between of the in the state of (if the grantor be married, insert the name of his wife) of the one part, and trustees, in trust for the uses and purposes hereinafter mentioned, all of the in the state of aforesaid, of the other part, WITNESSETH, that the said (if married, insert the name of his wife) for and in consideration of the sum of specie to in hand paid, at and upon the sealing and delivery of these presents, the receipt whereof is hereby acknowledged, hath (or have) given, granted, bargained, sold, released, confirmed, and conveyed, and by these presents doth (or do) give, grant, bargain, sell, release, confirm, and convey unto them, the said and their successors, (trustees in trust for the uses and purposes hereinafter mentioned and declared,) all the estate, right, title, interest, property claim, and demand whatsoever, either in law or equity, which he the said (if married, here insert the name of his wife) hath (or have) in, to, or upon all and singular a certain lot, or piece of land, situate, lying, and being in the and state aforesaid, bounded and butted as follows, to wit, (here insert the several courses and distances of the land to the place of beginning,) containing and laid out for acres of land, together with all and singular the houses, woods, waters, ways, privileges, and appurtenances thereto belonging, or in any wise pertaining: TO HAVE AND TO HOLD all and singular the above-mentioned and described lot or piece of land, situate, lying, and being as aforesaid, together with all and singular the houses, woods, waters, ways, and privileges thereto belonging, or in any wise appertaining unto them the said and their successors in office for ever in trust, that they shall erect and build, or cause to be erected and built thereon, a house or place of worship for the use of the members of the Methodist Episcopal Church in the United States of America, according to the rules and discipline which from time to time may be agreed upon and adopted by the ministers and preachers of the said Church at their General Conferences in the United States of America; and in further trust and confidence that they shal. at all times, for ever hereafter, permit such ministers and preachers belonging to the said Church, as shall from time to time be duly authorized by the General Conferences of the ministers and preachers of the said Methodist Episcopal Church, or by the annual conferences authorized by the said General Conference, to preach and expound God's holy word therein; and in further trust and confidence, that as often as any one or more of the trustees herein before mentioned shall die, or cease to be a member or members of the said Church according to the rules and discipline as aforesaid, then and in such case it shall be the duty of the stationed minister or preacher (authorized as aforesaid) who shall have the pastoral charge of the members of the said Church, to call a meeting of the remaining trustees as soon as conveniently may be: and when so met, the said minister or preacher shall proceed to nominate one or more persons to fill the place or places of him or them whose office or offices has (or have) been vacated as aforesaid. *Provided,* the person or persons so nominated shall have been one year a member or members of the said Church immediately preceding such nomination, and be at least twenty one years of age; and the said trustees, so assembled, shall proceed to elect, and by a majority of votes appoint, the person or persons so nominated to fill such vacancy or vacancies, in order to keep up the number of nine trustees for ever; and in case of an equal number of votes for and against the said nomination, the stationed minister or preacher shall have the casting vote.

Provided nevertheless, That if the said trustees, or any of them, or their successors, have advanced, or shall advance, any sum or sums of money, or are or shall be responsible for any sum or sums of money on account of the said premises, and they, the said trustees or their successors, be obliged to pay the said sums of money, they, or a majority of them, shall be authorized to raise the said sum or sums of money, by a mortgage on the said premises, or by selling the said premises, after notice given to the pastor or preacher who has the oversight of the congregation attending divine service on the said premises, if the money due be not paid to the said trustees, or their successors, within one year after such notice given; and if such sale take place, the said trustees, or their successors, after paying the debt and other expenses which are due from the money arising from such sale, shall deposit the remainder of the money produced by the said sale in the hands of the steward or stewards of the society belonging to or attending divine service on said premises; which surplus of the produce of such sale, so deposited in the hands of said steward or stewards, shall be at the disposal of the next annual conference author ized as aforesaid; which said annual conference shall dispose of the said money, according to the best of their judgment, for the use of the said society. And the said doth by these presents warrant, and for ever defend, all and singular the before-mentioned and described lot or piece of land, with the appurtenances thereto belonging unto them the said and their successors, chosen and appointed as aforesaid, from the claim or claims of him the said his heirs and assigns, and from the claim or claims of all persons whatever. In testimony whereof, the said (if married, insert the name of his wife) have hereto set their hands and seals, the day and year aforesaid.

Sealed and delivered in the presence of us (Two witnesses.)

Grantor's (L. S.)
his wife's (L. S.)

Received the day of the date of the above-written indenture, the consideration therein mentioned in full.

Witness.] Grantor's (L. S.)

County, ss.

Be it remembered, that on the day of in the year of our Lord one thousand personally appeared before me, one of the justices of the peace, in and for the county of and state of the within-named the grantor (if married, insert the name of his wife) acknowledged the within deed of trust to be their act and deed for the uses and purposes therein mentioned and declared; and she the said wife of the said being separate and apart from her said husband, by me examined, declared that she had made the same acknowledgment, freely and with her own consent, without being induced thereto through fear or threats of her said husband In testimony whereof I have hereto set my hand and seal, the day and year first above written.

Here the justice's name. (L. S.)

ALPHABETICAL INDEX.

COURSE OF STUDY

For Probationers and Travelling Deacons in the Methodist Episcopal Church.

FIRST YEAR.

The Bible—Doctrines.

The Existence of God; the Attributes of God, namely, Unity, Spirituality, Eternity, Omnipotence, Ubiquity, Omniscience, Immutability, Wisdom, Truth, Justice, Mercy, Love, Goodness, Holiness; the Trinity in Unity the Deity of Christ; the Humanity of Christ the Union of Deity and Humanity; Personality and Deity of the Holy Ghost; Depravity; Atonement; Repentance; Justification by Faith; Regeneration; Adoption; the Witness of the Spirit; Growth in Grace; Christian Perfection; Possibility of Final Apostasy; Immortality of the Soul; Resurrection of the Body; General Judgment; Rewards and Punishments.

[The examination on the above to be strictly Biblical, requiring the candidate to give the statement of the doctrine and the Scripture proofs. To prepare for this, he should read the Bible by course, and make a memorandum of the texts upon each of these topics as he proceeds.]

Systematic Divinity.

Watson's Institutes, First Part; Wesley's Plain Account of Christian Perfection.

Common English.

English Grammar; Modern Geography.

Composition.

Essay or Sermon.

[Read Wesley's Sermons and Notes; Watson's Life of Wesley; and Watson's Apology.]

SECOND YEAR.

The Bible—Sacraments.

The Sacrament of Baptism—Its Nature, Design, Obligation, Subjects, and Mode; The Sacrament of the Lord's Supper—Its Nature, Design, and Obligation.

[Mode of study and examination same as upon the Bible in the first year.]

Systematic Divinity

Watson's Institutes, Second Part; Peck's Christian Perfection, new 12mo. edition; Fletcher's Appeal.

Church Government.

Methodist Discipline; Stevens's Church Polity.*

Composition.

Essay or Sermon.

[Read Bishop Emory's Defence of our Fathers; Powell on Apostolical Succession; Dr. Emory's History of the Discipline; Wesley on Original Sin, and Wesley's Doctrinal Tracts; Johnston's Natural Philosophy.[*]]

THIRD YEAR.

The Bible—History and Chronology.

Candidates to be prepared upon the leading events recorded in the Old and New Testaments.

Reference Books: Horne's Introduction and Hibbard's Palestine.

Systematic Divinity.

Watson's Institutes, Third Part; Butler's Analogy; Peck's Rule of Faith;[*] Hibbard on Baptism.[*]

History, &c.

Ruter's Church History; Tytler's General History;[*] Newman's Rhetoric; Hedge's Logic.

Composition.

Essay or Sermon.

[Read Bangs's History of the Methodist Episcopal Church; Elliott on Romanism;[*] Fletcher's Works; Rollin's Ancient History;[*] Smith's Patriarchal Age; Hallam's Middle Ages;[*] Russell's Modern Europe.[*]]

FOURTH YEAR.

Review of the whole course.

Systematic Divinity.

Watson's Institutes, Fourth Part.

Preaching.

Claude's Essay on the Composition and Delivery of a Sermon.

Biblical Criticism.

Horne's Introduction, abridged.

Composition.

Essay or Sermon.

[Read Smith's Hebrew People; Mosheim's Ecclesiastical History; Townley's Illustrations of Biblical Literature; Watson's Sermons; History of the United States.]

* Those works in the course marked with an asterisk are optional with the annual conferences. Those so marked among the books to be read are recommended as highly important, but are not enjoined. The examination as to the other works required to be read, but not included in the course of study, shall extend only to the fact of reading

COURSE OF STUDY

Recommended for Local Preachers who are Candidates for Deacon's and Elder's Orders.

CANDIDATES FOR DEACON'S ORDERS.

The Bible—Doctrines.

The Existence of God; the Attributes of God, namely, Unity, Spirituality, Eternity, Omnipotence, Ubiquity, Omniscience, Immutability, Wisdom, Truth, Justice, Mercy, Love, Goodness, Holiness; the Trinity in Unity; the Deity of Christ; the Humanity of Christ; the Union of Deity and Humanity; Personality and Deity of the Holy Ghost; Depravity; Atonement; Repentance; Justification by Faith; Regeneration; Adoption; the Witness of the Spirit; Growth in Grace; Christian Perfection; Possibility of Final Apostasy; Immortality of the Soul; Resurrection of the Body; General Judgment; Rewards and Punishments.

The Bible—Sacraments.

The Sacrament of Baptism—Its Nature, Design, Obligation, Subjects, and Mode; the Sacrament of the Lord's Supper—Its Nature, Design, and Obligation.

[The examination on the above subjects is to be strictly Biblical, requiring the candidates to give the statement of the doctrine and the Scripture proofs. To prepare for this, he should read the Bible by course, and make a memorandum of the texts upon each of these topics as he proceeds.]

Systematic Divinity.

Watson's Institutes, Part First and Second; Wesley's Plain Account of Christian Perfection; Fletcher's Appeal.

Church Government.

Methodist Discipline.

Common English.

English Grammar; Modern Geography.

[Read Watson's Life of Wesley; Wesley's Sermons; Emory's Defence of our Fathers; Powell on Apostolical Succession.]

CANDIDATES FOR ELDER'S ORDERS.

Review of the previous course.

Bible—History.

The leading events recorded in the Old and New Testaments.

Systematic Divinity.

Watson's Institutes, Part Third and Fourth.

Composition.

An Essay or Sermon.

[Read Fletcher's Checks; Smith's Hebrew People; Ruter's Church History; Porter's Compendium of Methodism.]